The Ceramic Surface

The Ceramic Surface

Matthias Ostermann

A & C BLACK • LONDON

UNIVERSITY OF PENNSYLVANIA PRESS • PHILADELPHIA

First published in Great Britain 2002
A & C Black (Publishers) Limited
Alderman House
37 Soho Square
London W1D 3QZ
www.acblack.com

ISBN 0-7136-5427-9

Published simultaneously in the USA by
University of Pennsylvania Press
4200 Pine Street, Philadelphia
Pennsylvania 19104-4011

ISBN 0-8122-3701-3

Copyright © Matthias Ostermann 2002

A CIP catalogue record for this book is available
from the British Library and the US Library of Congress.

Matthias Ostermann has asserted his right under the Copyright, Design
and Patents Act, 1988, to be identified as the author of this work.

All rights reserved. No part of this publication may be reproduced in any
form or by any means – graphic, electronic or mechanical, including
photocopying, recording, taping or information storage and retrieval
systems – without the prior permission in writing from the publishers.

COVER ILLUSTRATIONS	From a selection of images shown in the book.
HALF TITLE	Plate: *Minotaur*
	[Coloured slips and sgraffito under transparent glaze]
FRONTISPIECE	Vessel: *First Encounter*
	[Earthenware with clay sgraffito, copper inlay and wash, vitreous engobes and coloured maiolica glaze]
	by Matthias Ostermann
	photograph by Jan Thijs

Cover design by Dorothy Moir
Book design by Penny and Tony Mills

A & C Black uses paper produced with elemental chlorine-free pulp,
harvested from managed sustainable forests.

Printed and bound in Singapore by Tien Wah Press Pte. Ltd

Contents

	Acknowledgements	vii
	Introduction	1
FOREWORD ONE:	Catherine Hess	5
	Superficial but not trivial	
	The Ceramic Surface from Past to Present	
FOREWORD TWO:	David Whiting	9
	Patterns of change	
	Ceramic Decoration in the Studio since the Second World War	
CHAPTER ONE	Manipulated clay surface	15
	Distorted, fragmented, thrown and altered, poured, pinched, coiled, cut, faceted, fluted, carved, press-mould additions, cut-out, incised, pierced, clay sgraffito, impressed, texture-paddled, eroded, stamped, sprigged, combed	
CHAPTER TWO	Colour in clay	43
	Clay mosaic, *neriage*, *nerikomi* (*millefiori*), lamination, lamination and slicing, poured coloured slips, clay inlay (*mishima*)	
CHAPTER THREE	Dry-surface decoration	55
	Stains and oxides, air-brushing, dry slips, terra sigillata, vitreous engobes, slip sgraffito and carving, slip inlay, layered slips and wiped-down glazes	
CHAPTER FOUR	Underglaze techniques	73
	Brushed, painted, poured, trailed, stippled, air-brushed coloured slips and underglaze colours under transparent and coloured glazes, cobalt and oxide painting under glaze, *hakeme* slip and sgraffito under glaze, sgraffito and carved slips under glaze, photocopying and serigraphic screenprinting under glaze	

CHAPTER FIVE	**Glazes used for effect**	97
	Brushed, painted, poured, trailed, sponge-printed and overlapped glazes, saturated colour glaze, underfired glaze, matt-surface glazes, crackle glaze, crystalline glaze, oil spot glaze, salt-glaze, crawling Shino glaze, raku glaze	
CHAPTER SIX	**In-Glaze painting**	113
	Maiolica: wet-blending and sgraffito, brush line-drawing, on-surface dry smudging, cobalt in-glaze painting, use of *coperta*, use of black underglaze, high-fire oxides	
CHAPTER SEVEN	**Resists and masking techniques**	125
	Shellac resists, wax, wax emulsion, *cuerda seca*, latex, paper stencils, tape resists	
CHAPTER EIGHT	**Third-firing on-glaze techniques**	145
	Oxidation lustre, lustre resists, reduction lustre, overglaze enamels (china paints), third-firing stains and sgraffito, transfers (decals), photo transfers and digitally manipulated imagery	
CHAPTER NINE	**Fire, smoke and ash surfaces**	165
	Raku firing, smoke firing and burnishing, Anagama firing and ash effects, wood-fired glaze effects	
CHAPTER TEN	**Unconventional approaches**	177
	Use of organic materials, use of found objects, use of non-ceramic materials (acrylics, urethane, detergent, wax), sand-blasted and eroded surfaces, acid-etching, faux-shards, gold leaf	
	Glossary of Terms and Techniques	196
	Recommended Reading	198
	Index	199

Acknowledgements

The pursuit of imagery and texts for this book has been a major part of the overall task, and many people have generously contributed their time and skills to make this book a reality.

For commissioning this book, and for on-going help and advice, thanks to Linda Lambert and Alison Stace of A & C Black Publishers in London, and for book design thanks to Penny Mills. For word-processing and constant support of my efforts to become computer-literate (not an easy task as I consider the computer as a modern drudgery rather than a creative toy), I would like to thank Alan Smith of Montreal. For proofreading, thanks to Sean McCutcheon in Montreal; for translations from the Spanish, to Concepción Cortacans in Montreal; and a special thanks to Dorothy Feibleman in London for translations from the Japanese.

For their very well researched and comprehensive essays in the foreword of this book, I am deeply grateful to Catherine Hess and to David Whiting.

For providing me with many of the contacts to the ceramists presented in this book, I would like to thank the following ceramists and authors in the United Kingdom: Peter Beard, Victoria and Michael Eden, Peter Ilsley, Peter Lane, Coll Minogue, Jane Perryman, Phil Rogers, Paul Scott, Ruthanne Tudball, Edmund de Waal and Jane Waller. Thanks also to Sam Jornlin and Lynn Peters in the United States, and to Evelyn Klam in Germany, Kevin White in Australia, Walter Ostrom in Canada and Moyra Elliott in New Zealand.

The following individuals, organisations and galleries have generously helped to provide contacts or have acted as intermediaries in providing me with imagery and texts: Anton Gallery in Washington, DC; Tom Aoyama at Coherence Inc. in Tokyo; Juliana Barrett at Barrett/Marsden Gallery in London; Anita Besson at Galerie Besson in London; Merlin Brooke-Little at Oxford Gallery in Oxford; Maria Antonia Casanovas, curator at the Museu de Ceràmica in Barcelona; Beatrice Chang at Dai Ichi Arts Ltd in New York; Sandra Chemske at Revolution Gallery in Ferndale, Michigan; Garth Clark, Mark Del Vecchio, Gretchen Atkins and Osvaldo Da Silva at Garth Clark Gallery in New York; Emmanuel Cooper at *Ceramic Review* in London; Gabi Dewald, editor-in-chief at *Keramikmagazin* in Germany; Marta Donaghey at Contemporary Ceramics in London; Helen Drutt Gallery in Philadelphia; Leslie Ferrin at Ferrin Gallery in Lenox, Massachusetts; Kate Gardiner and Janet Mansfield at *Ceramics: Art and Perception* in Sydney, Australia; Hanne Gørtz at Gallery Nørby in Copenhagen; Suzann Greenaway and David Kaye at Prime Gallery in Toronto; Laura Hamilton at Collins Gallery in Glasgow; The Hart Gallery in London; Sue Jefferies at The George R. Gardiner Museum of Ceramic Art in Toronto; Masahiro Karasawa, curator at Aichi Prefectural Museum in Japan; Christina Kohler at Bayrischer Kunstgewerbe Verein E.V. in Munich; Maureen Littleton Gallery in Washington, DC; Frank Lloyd Gallery in Santa Monica, California; Loes and Reinier International Ceramics in Deventer, the Netherlands; Melissa Longhi at the American Crafts Council in New York; Connie Love at Gail Severn Gallery in Ketchum, Idaho; Nancy Margolis Gallery in New York; Linda Ross at Sybaris Gallery, in Royal Oak, Michigan; Viscopy (Image Rights) in Australia; Eckard Wagner at the Emslandmuseum in Schloss Cemenswerth, Germany; and Renate Wunderle at Galerie B-15 in Munich.

Special thanks to Garth Clark in New York, to Helen Drutt in Philadelphia and to Shigenobu Kimura in Japan, for permission to use excerpts from their published texts.

Thanks also to the following ceramicists for providing technical information: Rob Barnard, Curtis Benzle, Peter Callas, Bruce Cochrane, Clare Conrad, Greg Daly, Thomas Hoadley, Ron Roy, Paul Scott, Christopher Staley, Sasha Wardell, Eric Wong and Roswitha Wulff.

Last, but not least, my heartfelt thanks go to all the ceramicists whose imagery and texts have made this book possible.

Introduction

When first contemplating this book as a project, I rather simplistically viewed it as a compilation of images of the work of contemporary ceramists specialising in surface decoration. To my surprise, once I started approaching people around the world for images of their work, I found that many do not see themselves as 'decorators', with the perhaps implicit definition of light-weight on-surface patterning. Most of them, in fact, approach the ceramic surface with the same vigour and inventiveness that they apply to their research into form, function, spatial values, narrative, etc., and the final surface treatments are an integral part of the total concept of work. I decided at that point that the book needed to deal with the ceramic surface in all of its variety and configurations, and that of course opened up so huge a field of study that somewhere a limiting framework needed to be established. The imagery and information in this book deal largely (with some loose exceptions) with those ceramic works whose primary mandate is the exploration of vessel and platter forms, and their treatment over approximately the last decade of the 20th century. I have certainly included non-functional and at times even sculpturally-oriented works, but I have avoided the categories of figurative sculpture, architectural ceramics and installation works. These have been thoroughly and specifically addressed by other ceramic authors. Within my chosen framework I have pursued those images that present the fullest possible scope of surface treatment in all its variety. Although I have not closed my eyes to the importance of form and content in a given work, my primary preoccupation in this book is with the 'skin' of the work, and the immediate (often first) visual response to surface, be it textural, colourful, traditionally inspired, unconventional, provocative – yet always integral to the maker's purpose.

It was in fact difficult to find work to exclude, since every ceramic object has some kind of deliberate outer surface treatment. However, where I felt that the focus of expression in a work dealt primarily with form and spatial values, and surface treatment was minimal, I did not pursue that work in this context. Nor have I provided an overall view of the history of the ceramic surface, since that

Vase detail: *The Staircase* by Matthias Ostermann
[Maiolica with dry-blended stains and sgraffito]
Photograph by Jan Thijs

would cover such a vast field of knowledge in itself. Pots have been embellished in all ceramic-making cultures from Neolithic times to the present day, and many books have explored this subject in great detail. I do provide, however, two interesting points of view in the joint foreword to this book, in the form of two essays. Catherine Hess of the United States provides a broad historical overview of the development of decorated ceramics and cross-cultural influences up to the 20th century, and David Whiting of the United Kingdom gives us a contemporary perspective on the movements and changes influencing the approach to ceramic surface decoration in the period since the Second World War.

Once all the imagery was assembled, I was most impressed by the great diversity of techniques inherent in the medium of ceramics. Few other materials allied to the making process can boast such an enormous scope of creative expression as do clay and glaze. What to me is most exciting is that regardless of whether a particular surface treatment is influenced by past traditions, rebels against it, or is totally newly invented – it always remains intensely personal, an intimate visual testimony to an artist's particular chosen road. It is my belief that there are not just one or two important languages of communication here, but rather many, each having its own particular place and following, and each contributing to the overall family of languages that embrace all possible forms of expression.

The book is organised into ten chapters, each covering what I believe to be a specific technique category that embraces all types of clay, methods of construction, temperatures and firing procedures. Few ceramic works are so simple as to fall into just one category – most are a deliberate combination of applied specialised and compatible techniques. I have attempted (rightly or wrongly) for the sake of some kind of order to place each object into that category which (to my eye) gives it an immediate visual focus and particular expression. Most often I have tried to let the artists themselves choose their own categories. Each image is accompanied by two texts, again provided by the artists themselves. One gives a procedural, technical description of the work, and the other (to me equally important) is a personal statement giving insight into the motivation, the inspiration behind that particular work; the starting point of the whole process. I think that we as ceramicists are, by necessity, problem solvers, and hence we will readily absorb technical information. However, the moving spirit behind the work is more difficult to express and to grasp, yet to my mind, just as necessary to the true understanding of any work, and to the essential dialogue occurring between maker and viewer. That dialogue is of course the *raison d'être* of any work of art created.

Not to be found in this book are glaze recipes, appendices, technical charts and graphs, providing specific problem-solving information. These are not my forte and have been better covered by other authors. However, a glossary of terms and techniques is provided at the end of this book, followed by a list of recommended reading of a technical, aesthetic and philosophic nature. I hope that enough information has been provided throughout to stimulate the readers' curiosity and their appetite for further research and experimentation.

I have tried to keep the scope of this book as international as possible, and regret that many countries are under-represented, or not represented at all, merely due to my lack of access to the right sources of information within the time allotted for publication. Above and beyond all of its possible shortcomings, the purpose of this book is to provide readers (be they artists, students, educators or historians) with a guide to the many techniques and varied approaches used today in the treatment of the ceramic surface.

This book is, quite simply, a celebration of the ingenuity and diversity of making skills of all the ceramicists included here.

Matthias Ostermann

Montreal, 2002

Maiolica Dish from Deruta, d. 32cm (12 ½ in.). c. 1530
Courtesy of the George R. Gardiner Museum of Ceramic Art, Toronto

foreword one

Superficial but not trivial

The Ceramic Surface from Past to Present

Why are we compelled to decorate our objects, our surroundings, ourselves? And how do we choose that decoration? Certainly, our cultural and social environment (where we live and whom we live with, what we do and whom we emulate) influences our decisions. What our forebears chose must affect these decisions as well. It also seems likely that how our brain functions has something to do with what we want to touch, handle, look at, use. Beyond that, individual choice is as elusive a subject as is why we find one thing attractive and another not.

Ceramics are known to have been produced for at least 10,000 years. If not the oldest, they are certainly among the oldest products of human manufacture. The reasons for this are simple. They are made from materials (clay, minerals, ash, sand) that are both widespread and accessible. They are easily shaped by hand, on a wheel, or in a mould, and hardened with air and fire. Finally, and arguably most significantly, ceramic objects are essentially utilitarian.

This idea of usefulness is not a restricted one. It encompasses the servicing of any human activity including the spiritual, the commemorative, the political, the social, and the personal. The scope of these objects includes votive figures as well as food, drug, and drink containers; religious plaques as well as inkwells and flower vases; architectural tiles, as well as dining ware. As other crafts and industries developed (i.e. metallurgy, glassblowing, plastic manufacture) to create the objects needed for daily life, the exigencies of clay to form useful things abated and the more expressive nature of the medium began to be exploited.

First among these 'expressive' embellishments is the choice and handling of the clay itself. The visual, tactile, and auditory differences among high-fired or low-fired, coarse or fine, dark- or light-coloured clay bodies set the stage and partly determine any other ornamentation. Historically, this choice, where a choice could be made, was determined by changing taste and economics. For example, in 15th-century Italy, once collectors saw porcelain (arriving, as it was, from the East) they wanted it. In 18th-century England, creamware – developed as a cheaper alternative to porcelain – became all the rage, driving out of business earthenware and porcelain factories alike. Common in China in the 4th century, stoneware was first widely produced in the West in only one area: the Rhineland region of Germany in the late Middle Ages. The reason for this circumscribed popularity was not accidental but arose from the local availability of the necessary raw materials for stoneware's production as well as its appeal to local clients. In the 17th century, Chinese red stoneware arrived in the Netherlands and England where it was imitated. Around 1710, its subsequent manufacture by J.F. Böttger at Meissen led to the creation of the first hard paste porcelain of the West.

After the choice of the clay, the prime arena for ceramic expression is the object's very surface. Aside from practical alterations (glazing to make a pot watertight or roughening a pot's surface to better grasp it) all other surface treatments are ornamental: made to inform the eye and hand rather than to modify function. The scope of surface treatments is broad, limited only by available materials and by the physics of ceramic production.

Indeed, fluctuations of decorative style are greatly determined by the developments of technique. The interest in celebrating classical knowledge and in rendering one's spatial environment with precision influenced the Renaissance potters' desire to learn and further expand the medium of tin-glazed earthenware, or maiolica. From the Middle Ages, the technique travelled with Islamic craftsmen from the Eastern Mediterranean across North Africa to Spain and, then, by the 15th century, to Italy. Lead glazes are harder to control and are less vividly colourful than the glazes that are produced by adding tin oxide to the mix. The presence of tin allows the glaze to be stable as well as bright white. As a result, the painted pigments on this glaze ground appear most colourful and do not blur or run when fired. This decorative technique made possible the depiction of narrative scenes as extensions of the viewers' world, that is, with naturalistic elements subtly modelled and placed within linear perspective: a hallmark of Renaissance painting in fresco, and on panel, canvas, and vellum.

The lustre technique followed much the same route. Lustreware became much sought after in Renaissance Italy, though the challenging process of its manufacture was mastered in only a few towns. Certainly, its high value resulted as much from the difficulty and labour-intensity of its production as from its association with precious metals. By the late 16th century, it passed from vogue. It was even ignored by other European potteries while its parent, tin-glazed technique was becoming ever more popular. Lustre only appeared again in the 19th century when it was revived by William de Morgan and others seeking to evoke the exoticism of Islamic lustres, and also the luxuriance of turn-of-the-century art nouveau. It has remained popular, with some artists, such as Alan Caiger-Smith (interested in its Islamic roots), while others, such as Beatrice Wood, concern themselves more with its luxuriant sensuality.

The attraction to the exotic was also at the heart of porcelain's appeal. Indeed, the chromatic coupling of blue and white decoration (on earthenware as well as porcelain) was always to some degree associated with its precursor: Chinese Ming porcelain dating from the late 14th century. However, the decoration struck a chord with collectors who seem to have appreciated it as much for its simplicity and intensity of colour, as for its exotic birth.

Whether the availability of techniques determines the styles of ceramic ornamentation or whether the decorative idea drives discovery of technique may be issues that are impossible to disentangle from one another. Certainly the development of hard paste porcelain production – with its capability of creating objects whose shape and decoration belie their creation by human hands – was perfectly suited to its luxury clients, fond of the current restrained yet exquisite Rococo style. This production was meant to impress the viewer with *tour-de-force* technique, a decorative effect that was only possible in this particular medium.

In the early 20th century, the interest in featuring physical materials, strength of form, and simplicity of decoration influenced Shoji Hamada's decision to use stoneware and earthenware clays, in order to feature the object's organic and natural character. This interest, together with the celebration of the handmade, was fundamental to the studio pottery movement involving such ceramists as Bernard Leach and his followers in the United Kingdom and the English-speaking world.

Today, ceramic surfaces are as myriad as the techniques that engender them. Colour can be painted, trailed, stained or otherwise applied with pigments, coloured slips, coloured glazes and cold paint. The ceramicist can choose among the subtlety of underglaze, the brilliance of in-glaze, or the precision of overglaze decoration. Inscribed patterns or burnished surfaces appeal to the hand as well as to the eye. Surface texture and pigmentation can be varied through the use of salt, ash, metallic oxides and other materials fired in ways that differ according to the temperature reached and the amount of oxygen present. Even unwanted firing results (such as flashing or crazing) can be purposefully used to decorative effect.

The ease with which clay is formed and made permanent has made possible the economical and efficient production of functional ware for thousands of years, and the availability of the materials for surface decoration has made possible experimentation and innovation in this area. Indeed, few other media are able to produce such varied effects. In the past, the materials and know-how on hand have exerted a strong influence on resulting styles. Today, however, this is less the case. The ever increasing number of technologies and materials at the potter's disposal suggest that the future holds some surprises.

Catherine Hess
January 2001

Catherine Hess is Associate Curator, Department of Sculpture and Works of Art, J. Paul Getty Museum, Los Angeles, California.

Peter Voulkos (United States)

Untitled Plate, w. 53.5 cm (21 in.), 1998. Fired in Peter Callas Kiln, New Jersey
Surface: Wheel-thrown and altered stoneware, high-fired reduction.

This plate was wheel-thrown and altered, using a stoneware body, one half of which was a *kenosei* (Japanese local clay). The variegated surface is a result of ash interaction with the clay surface, from a prolonged Anagama wood firing (up to seven days), with an equal cooling time. Final firing temperature was approximately 1320–1360°C (2408–2480°F). Careful heat monitoring was required towards the end of the firing to avoid denaturalising of ash.

Photograph: Schopplein Studio, S.F.
Courtesy of Private Collection, Japan

A pot, for me, is a vessel that has an opening, that you can see inside, that can receive. If it is a good pot, it also has some sculptural qualities involved with space and form. Most of the forms I make refer to pottery. Maybe that makes me a potter. The utilitarian aspect doesn't interest me though. It doesn't mean much, but maybe the best label is 'Abstract Expressionist' if that means that I have to get my hands into my material before I know exactly where I am going. I am not a conceptual artist. I can't just sit there and think of an idea. Most of it just comes out of my hands. I have always used whatever comes to hand, or into my head, that makes sense in my own work – that I can get some energy from.

From 'Peter Voulkos Talking; A Transcription,' statement by the artist edited by Bill Woodcock, c. 1981–82, in the artist's collection

foreword two

Patterns of change

CERAMIC DECORATION IN THE STUDIO SINCE THE SECOND WORLD WAR

In the last 100 years, the culture of ceramic decoration has been a pluralistic carnival, and even more so in the last 50, as the number of potters and their personal credos has increased. In contrast to the vibrant, but essentially static, traditions indigenous to certain societies, the studio movement (by its very nature) is an aesthetic magpie, attempting to find a language and articulation of surface as expressive as the form of the pot itself, indeed often more so. The story of post-war ceramics is the story of a highly concentrated, increasingly frenetic search for innovation and change, often for its own sake. Such individuality is just as marked in the dogged independence of repetition throwers (who may plead a kind of creative anonymity) as it is in the work of ceramic 'artists', their approach to form and surface drawing just as revealing of philosophy and intention.

Perhaps we recognise potters less by their forms and more by their colour and punctuation of that surface, the 'coating' of the object, an integral part of its communicative function. At its best, the expression of surface becomes a visually and physically tactile experience, integrated into the very body of the pot, an extension of its spirit, to use a very Leachian phrase. At its worst, decoration can be merely that, an applied wallpaper in which the 'canvas' of the pot is secondary, a tendency often emphasised by the blank banality of what we find inside. It is very sad that decoration can become a means by which we can totally control the clay – eliminating its natural properties by swamping it in pattern-making that suggests a dominance, rather than intuitive reading of the material. Decoration is often more to do with matters of 'style' and 'design' than expressive liberation.

In considering the bewildering spectrum of post-war adornment, it is useful to think about the new availability of information in the years following that conflict. Such works as Bernard Leach's *A Potter's Book*, Arthur Lane's *Style in Pottery* and W. B. Honey's *The Art of the Potter* all appeared in the 1940s, as did the new, highly significant, Faber monographs on pottery and porcelain. Whatever else they were, such publications became influential style manuals for budding potters, as did the new ceramic magazines directed to studio makers, which became widely available by the 1960s and 1970s. Their import was, of course, as visual and aesthetic as it was technical, often more so. The increasingly copious choice of illustrations (in the early days confined to black and white) were a heady introduction to the three-dimensional world of museums. Public collections became an important resource for the new (albeit uneven) ceramic courses being slowly established in the art colleges. In these galleries, as in the micro-cultures of individual books, were concentrated readings of ceramic history from which students could glean; painted Cretan vessels, lustred Persian wares, engraved Chinese and Korean stonewares, energetically trailed English slipware, pre-Columbian pots, and of course the elaborate heritage of the European factories. The list was endless.

We have to remind ourselves of the obvious fact that when we look at the decoration of Pre-Industrial wares, particularly those of the indigenous traditions, we are studying types of elaboration often imbued with the history, ritual and religious beliefs of particular societies, just as form was itself dictated by specific function and use. A potter's excitement in studying such embellishments today will, generally speaking, lie less in their anthropological significance and more in what can be gleaned for his or her formal and stylistic purposes. As I wrote recently, in comparing our 20th-century studio work to ceramic traditions in Africa: 'Modern European ceramics (for example) are marginalised objects, whether we like it or not. Most people use their pottery unconsciously. With that central role lost, we have to allude to their properties of tactility, domestic enrichment or expressive power in artists' statements and critical discourse. Our words support our actions. In studio ceramics, it is a battle of individual credos, a stylistic steeplechase.'[1] As I then went on to say, 'style' has become an end in itself and decoration, after all, can be read as just that, though there are many potters (including the author of this book) whose symbolic and narrative imagery is implicit. It is inseparable from a vessel's deeper meaning.

So, what kind of picture do we have of the decorative landscape in 1945? It began with its limitations. Source material, such as *A Potter's Book* with its Anglo-Oriental bias, was always valuable but often prescriptive. Bernard Leach's vision was passionate, its Ruskinian belief in materials persuasive. This was a world of the quietest ash and tenmoku glazes, of lyrical painting and incising on traditional orientally-inspired forms. It was a decoration of brevity and understatement – a style replicated, sometimes with individual spirit, by countless followers in search of an artistic direction. However, it could be said, that, despite the omnipotence of the Leach School (its influence felt in the

---

[1] Review of *Ten Thousand Years of Pottery* by Emmanuel Cooper, *Crafts* No. 165, July/August 2000.

USA, Canada, Scandinavia, New Zealand, Australia), it was quite insular. After all, it derived most of its ideas from the history of ceramics itself. In this sense it was, to some degree, self-absorbed. There were alternatives. In London, William Newland of the Central School, was, from 1949, teaching a liberated aesthetic that looked beyond ceramics. He admired early European and Mediterranean pottery, but also looked to the artistic avant-garde of painting and sculpture in France. His gestural slip-decorated earthenware and the vibrant tin glaze of Nicholas Vergette, Margaret Hine and James Tower (the 'Picassiettes' as Leach derisively dubbed them) were more in tune with Picasso's ceramic work at Vallauris, and experiments in the United States, than home-grown traditions.

In prosperous post-war America the crafts were now being widely taught in art colleges. Though Leach's influence was strongly felt (through his lecture tours as well as his writings), a far more sculptural direction was soon being taken by Peter Voulkos and Paul Soldner, where surfaces were energised by expressionist painting and exciting textures. It all seemed far removed from the smoothly elegant sgraffito of Austrian-born Lucie Rie in England (a decoration which quietly emphasised and delineated the design of her pots) or the equally Modernist forms of Karl and Ursula Scheid in Germany, with their muted glazes animated by resist. However, Rie's work could be monumental in scale and her glazes elemental and volcanic. The German refugee Hans Coper developed a vocabulary of texture and form where additional embellishment was unnecessary, a far cry from the elegantly oriental brushwork of William Staite Murray in the 1930s, or Michael Cardew's revival of English slipware. Ultimately, Rie, Coper and the Scheids were children of the Bauhaus legacy.

Scandinavian ceramics also felt the reverberations of central European modernism. Studio production had long collaborated with industry, but in the 1950s and 1960s many individual potters emerged, working solely in their studios. What was obvious about the work of Wilhelm Kage in Sweden and Christian Poulsen in Denmark were their historically resonant elemental forms and deep luminous glazes, continued today in the work of the Turkish-born Dane, Alev Siesbye. If there was, generally speaking, a comparable austerity in some Canadian and Antipodean ceramics, resulting from Leach's influence, America's expressive experimentation gained momentum. By the mid 1960s, it had become distinctly baroque and at its worst, nothing short of ceramic kitsch, in fact a word that would have delighted many of the new 'Funk' artists. Born out of Pop Art, Funk straddled the boundaries of good taste, but its message was serious enough. Often crudely modelled and painted, it drew on popular imagery and politics to make its statements. Robert Arneson, pupil of Voulkos and a leading figure, painted on watery slips which added more colour than depth to his surfaces, but his legacy was a powerful one. He helped lay the foundations for a ceramic culture where decorative excess was the name of the game, a state of affairs only accelerated by the flimsy tenets of Post Modernism, and the global spread of its shock tactics, even to the misty reaches of the Orient. Of course Japan had already gone avant-garde, at least partially, just after the war. Though the Mingei-inspired ceramics of Hamada, Tomimoto and Kawai remained influential, the 'Sodeisha' movement in Tokyo (established in 1948) produced Western orientated sculptural work in response to the contemporary issues of a country adjusting to a new post-war climate. Colour and decoration were often excessive, even disturbing, a challenging response to the turmoil and confusion of a fast industrialising society.

So, how does the land lie today? In an age when visual information is there at the touch of a button, and when craft appears to have merged into art, the definitions are complex, the boundaries ambiguous. To over-simplify the situation, one can identify three general areas of activity; first, the production of time-honoured functional wares for the table; second, the making of more decorative objects for domestic enrichment; and third, purely sculptural work, where the clay is used primarily for expressive ends. In the field of function, there appears to have been a reaction, in the 1990s, to the glitzy decor and vivid colour of the 1970s and 1980s (itself a rebellion, to some extent, against Leachian sobriety). You could call it a return to basics manifested in a widening interest in the properties of salt-glaze, in other traditional kiln techniques such as wood firing, and the emergence of a new minimalist porcelain, with its roots as much in industrial design as craft pottery and post-Bauhaus aesthetics.

The second region of activity, that which the perceptive critic Michael Robinson called 'ornamentalist' has been aesthetically problematic. Potters working to produce *objets* for display rather than functional use, have often produced work of great quality, but it is, it has to be said, an area of variable quality. The use of more integrated and traditionalist decorative methods (impressing, stamping, sgraffito, etc.) have often achieved a more convincing marriage of body and surface, but the ubiquity of misappropriated elaboration, used to excess, remains a menace in contemporary practice. An overuse of resists, inlays, stencils, lustres, gilding and other techniques can lead to an overworking of surface that leaves form quite secondary. Some ceramists positively delight in such an approach, but it leaves those of a more 'Ruskinian' bent lamenting the polarisation of the bone of the pot from its skin, the loss of material vigour and a proper appreciation of the 'three-dimensional' nature and complexity of ceramics.

Personal hobby horses aside, there is much to celebrate on the contemporary scene. The third area of pursuit, that of sculpture, is at its best, very exciting today. It has done most to look beyond the boundaries of ceramics for its impetus and direction, and because it has largely moved away from the concept of the vessel, has found it easiest to move on. Again, geology and process have been important properties for those who inherited the language of 1950s and 1960s hand construction, many of whom we can call, to borrow Garth Clark's phrase, 'organic abstractionists'. An important aspect in the history of modern clay building has been the integration of colour, texture and form, the need to make body and surface one, a kind of elemental fusion. Decoration as such has become superfluous. Or, at least we have to broaden our definition of what decoration means. Today many ceramists prefer the serendipitous fabric of nature in their pots, implicit to their *raison d'être* as artists using clay. There is equally good figuration about, where strong painting and glazing has done much to enliven form (and often with great wit as well as pathos) but for many ceramists, the question lies less in where to start, and more in where to stop.

Certainly, after the Post-Modernist 1980s, when ceramics, like so much else, played fast and loose, the situation appears to be a calmer one. There is still much of the Baroque about, much of this decadence inventive and delicious, but one is aware of how the materials themselves are back on the agenda. There is a return to a kind of physicality, where for many artists, the residue of the object's creation is integral to its aesthetic. Of course this approach can also be taken too far. The 'anonymous' actions of nature are actually another form of assertive self-expression, and pots drowning in treacly fly ash can be self-indulgent and mannered. Remember the song 'Mud, mud, glorious mud'? Generally speaking though, this return to a material culture is to be welcomed, if it allows the clay itself to speak more openly. It would be good to see a touch more alchemy in the discipline, or as I put it once, 'romantic deviance'. It was the late ceramic sculptor Ewen Henderson who, concerned with our tendency to 'tinker' in pottery, to smother and sterilise it with concepts, urged us to move on. As he wrote in a recent letter; 'The visual arts have become too involved in ideas. I feel that essence precedes idea, and that if you can succeed in making essence, you can hang most ideas on it like a spare jacket . . . of course you cannot deny ideas-based art, but I think the see-saw is stuck down on one side, and I would like to see it going up and down again.' Not bad words, those.

David Whiting
December 2000

David Whiting is a writer and critic in the applied arts. The son of noted British potter Geoffrey Whiting, he is a contributor to a number of magazines in the applied arts field, including Crafts *(United Kingdom) and* Ceramics: Art and Perception *(Australia).*

chapter one
Manipulated clay surface

Manipulated clay surface deals with those ceramic objects that have active clay surface intervention. Here perhaps the making process will be most evident, and although (as mentioned in the Introduction) few works fall into only one simple category, the pieces illustrated in this chapter have been chosen for their initial visual impact of exploited three-dimensional surfaces including: distortion, fragmentation, throwing and altering, pouring, pinching, coiling, cutting, faceting, fluting, carving, addition of press-moulded segments, surface cut-outs, incising, piercing, clay sgraffito, impressing, texture-paddling, clay erosion, stamping, sprigging and combing. These techniques are used in conjunction with all types of clays, firing temperatures and firing methods.

Wendy Walgate (Canada)

Wall Plate (detail), w. 48 cm (19 in.), 1996.

Surface: Press-moulded relief additions. Earthenware, coloured glazes, low-fired, oxidation.

White low-fire clay with good 'tooth' was used to throw the initial plate form. Layered press-moulded pieces were added, these being directly taken from diverse objects, rather than using plaster moulds. The objects (plastic, glass, metal, ceramics, etc.) were coated with baking powder as a release mechanism. After bisquing, multiple glaze firings took place, using self-mixed and commercial coloured glazes. The work was fired in oxidation to 1040°C (1904°F).

Photograph: Wendy Walgate
Courtesy of Prime Gallery, Toronto

Interaction of form, colour and texture is a primary focus of my work. I use clay impressions taken from found objects that have some connection to my personal history, environment, and relationships. These objects can include disposable items such as cardboard florists' containers, old bicycle chains, discarded machinery and tools, broken toys, cast iron stove parts, ashtrays, condiment dishes, teeth and hand impressions, and used printing blocks. From these impressions, the present can be read in the disposable objects of today, the past in the personal objects from my childhood, and the future can be interpreted from the industrial, machine-like forms. Another intent of my work is to entertain and provide humour for the viewer. I like to include the qualities of playfulness, intrigue and a small element of intimidation in my work.

Wendy Walgate

Jean-François Fouilhoux (France)

Chassezac, 46 x 32 x 15.5 cm (18 x 12 ½ x 6 in.), 1997.

Surface: Dark-green celadon glaze over sculpted stoneware. High-fired, reduction.

This sculpture was hand modelled and manipulated, using stoneware clay. After bisquing, it was dipped into a dark-green celadon glaze, and fired in a downdraught gas kiln in reduction to 1250°C (2282°F).

Photograph: Jean-Jacques Morer

It is my interest in Chinese Sung Dynasty glazes that 'orients' my work. Nevertheless, no material exists without evidencing some kind of form or shape and in my work it is the shapes of shell and carapace-covered animals that inspire me. Like the ceramicist they create their own mineral covering. Why celadon? It is a marriage between material and light.

Jean-François Fouilhoux

Rudolf Staffel (United States)

Light Gatherer, h. 12.5 (5 in.), w. 9 cm (3 ½ in.), 1990.

Surface: Broken and reassembled wheelthrown porcelain. High-fired, oxidation.

This porcelain form was initially wheel-thrown, altered, broken and reassembled, with a partially eroded surface. It was treated with a light cobalt wash, and when dry, was once-fired in oxidation to 1200°C (2192°F). The very high firing, combined with varying wall thickness, creates varied and semi-translucent surfaces.

Photograph: George Erml
Courtesy of Helen Drutt Gallery, Philadelphia

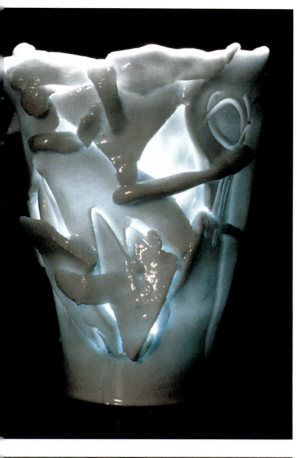

Painting seemed to create more anxiety. Working in clay was much more comfortable. First of all, working in clay is a primordial experience that is very, very comfortable. I think every infant has manipulated something that was soft and gushy and pleasurable to touch. Also, the effort of working in clay as a studio practice meant many, many hours of mechanical work, balancing the more cerebral and creative. In other words, there was that great attraction for the physical activity of preparing to be an artist, which lessened the anxiety of wondering whether or not one was being properly creative, which I think almost all people who go through the arts experience in their early maturing years.

Rudolf Staffel
Interview with the artist for the 'Archives of American Art,'
conducted by Helen Williams Drutt English, July 16, 1987, in Philadelphia

Julian A. Jadow (United States)

Untitled, h. 30 cm (11 ¾ in.), w. 12 cm (4 ¾ in.), 1997.

Surface: Straw-coloured slab-wrapped cylinder. High-fired stoneware, reduction.

This vase form was thrown using a clay body that bisque fires to a light grey. A thin slab was rolled out, and the surface of the cylinder and one surface of the slab were combed with clay slip. The slab was then torn and draped about the cylinder form. After bisquing, a matt straw-coloured glaze was sprayed over and the piece was fired in reduction to 1300°C (2372°F).

Photograph: Benjamin Dimmit
Courtesy of Gallery Dai Ichi Arts Ltd, New York

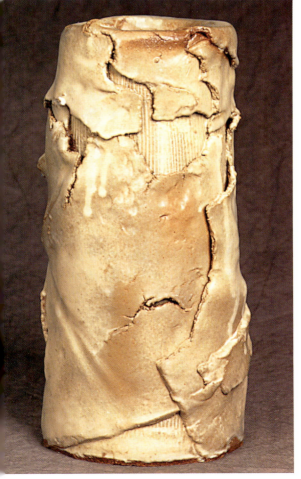

The Japanese potter Sakuma has been a major influence on my work. My early work was traditional in shape and glaze, and in its precise but relaxed simplicity was characteristic of Japanese pottery. In recent years, I have begun to experiment with altered original forms with a range of glaze surfaces from liquid washes to grainy mists. Other work where the clay is draped and folded over an underlying shape results in a deconstructed form having an appearance slightly against the grain of its expected look.

Julian A. Jadow

Chris Staley (United States)

Porcelain Vessel on Black Plate, h. 20 cm (8 in.), w. 33 cm (13 in.), 1994.

Surface: Contrasted thrown celadon porcelain with torn black fire clay. High-fired, reduction.

The porcelain vessel was loosely thrown, using a rib to create a relaxed undulating outer surface. After bisquing, it was celadon-glazed and fired in gas reduction to 1300°C (2372°F). The plate was slabbed and torn, using a black stoneware fire clay, and salt-fired in reduction to 1260°C (2300°F). The water-like soft porcelain surface contrasts strongly with the raw, earthy, almost elemental black fire clay.

Photograph: Dick Ackley

For me the essence of making pots is about being human; fragility and strength, the intimate moment when the handle of a cup touches the hand. Pots are about potential. Pots can create a world of slow time where meaning can be found. It is a notable experience to use pots that exude the soul of the maker. All of our senses are engaged in this experience. Very few things can be touched and leave one a different person. It is the paradox of who is touching whom that gives pots their greatest potential.

Chris Staley

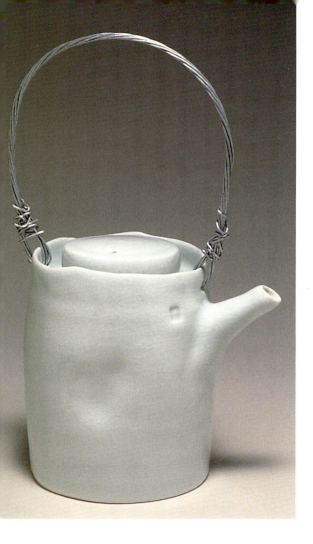

Edmund de Waal (United Kingdom)

Teapot, h. 15 cm (6 in.), 2000.

Surface: Thrown, distorted and stamped porcelain. High-fired celadon glaze, reduction.

This porcelain teapot was loosely wheel-thrown and trimmed with deliberate handling and distortion marks left on the surface, as well as a small stamped pattern. After bisquing, it was dipped in a celadon glaze and gas fired in reduction to 1300°C (2372°F).

Photograph: Sara Morris

Porcelain is an odd material to work with. Is it precious, or just expensive? It occupies a curiously charged area – the material for palaces, the pivot of Oriental trade, a cipher for 'Eastern-ness'; it is a value-laden material enveloped with history, and sometimes gilt mounts. In contemporary studio ceramics it is most visible as the perfect poised and translucent 'don't touch' bowl. But for me there is another canon of porcelain-making that is also vivid. There are the stacks of cream glazed dishes so common in provincial French homes. There is the fiercely white functional porcelain designed by Henry Cole, and there are the old Korean celadons so prized in Japan; with their washed-out colours, warped bowls, slumped bottles, cracked jars mended with rivets or with gold. This is porcelain that can be lived with and handled; kitchen porcelain.

Edmund de Waal

Shigekazu Nagae (Japan)

Vessel with Thin Layers, h. 15.5 cm (6 in.), w. 51 cm (20 in.), 1999.

Surface: Dripped porcelain slip into drape mould. High-fired, oxidation.

This vessel was made using the *otoshikomi* technique of drip-casting which involved small amounts of slip being trailed in linear patterns into geometric-shaped plaster moulds over a few hours. After 12 hours, the process was repeated to complete wall thicknesses and to create a delicate woven effect. Once dry, the piece was bisqued with strategic supports to encourage soft warping, and after bisquing, several layers of feldspathic glaze were dripped over with a spatula and rubbed back down. The piece was fired to 1300°C (2372°F).

Photograph: Shigeru Akimoto

I grew up with a family ceramic business whose concern was to create vessels for daily use, employing casting techniques. Since such techniques in Japan were viewed as 'commercial' and not 'artistic', I decided to use my acquired casting skills to invent a wholly new type of slipcast work that defies standard definition and can be perceived as a unique ceramic art form in its own right.

Shigekazu Nagae

Masamichi Yoshikawa (Japan)

Kayho, 35 x 35 x 17 cm (13 ¾ x 13 ¾ x 6 ¾ in.), 2000.

Surface: Cut, carved and hand-modelled slab construction. High-fired porcelain, reduction.

Using *Amakusa* and New Zealand porcelain, this piece was assembled from soft-cut slabs and pieces with minimal use of tools, and hand-imprinted and manipulated while the clay was still soft. The solid-walled piece was encased in a brick structure, and slowly bisque-fired over five or six days in an electric kiln. A celadon glaze was then brushed on and the piece was gas fired in reduction to 1310°C (2390°F).

Photograph: Thomoki Fujii

My work deals with the simplicity and spontaneity of visible gesture in the making process, to provoke an emotional response from the viewer. The hand print evokes the here and now, forever visible in the fired clay, the celadon glaze is reminiscent of flowing water – one of life's basic ever-present necessities.

Masamichi Yoshikawa

Maria Bofill (Spain)

Labyrinth, 23 x 23 x 6.5 cm (9 x 9 x 2 ½ in.), 2000.

Surface: Slab-constructed and pinched porcelain. High-fired, reduction.

This sculpture was slab-built, using a high-molochite porcelain clay. Once joined, the shape walls were finely pinched. After bisquing to 980°C (1796°F), the piece was gas fired in reduction to 1300°C (2372°F), blue slip and transparent glaze were added and a third firing took place in oxidation to 1200°C (2192°F). A final gold lustre firing to 815°C (1499°F) completed the piece.

Photograph: Maria Bofill

I enjoy working on the ancient symbol of the labyrinth, with its world of perspective and the dialectic engendered between the wall and the emptiness the wall surrounds. My works are reflections about the urban and the imaginary landscape, seen from the point of view of small Mediterranean architectures, which may be seen as real or not.

Maria Bofill

Kim Dickey (United States)

Stacked Salad Bowl Set with Pepper Shaker, h. 25.5 cm (10 in.), w. 30.5 cm (12 in.), 1998.
Surface: Hand-pinched porcelain construction. High-fired, reduction.

This set of objects was constructed from porcelain, hand-pinching upward from a solid base of clay, adding material in an intuitive way, until completion. Coloured glazes were applied by dipping, pouring and brushing, and the set was fired with residual salt in a downdraught gas kiln to 1260°C (2300°F).

Photograph: Kim Dickey

I've been intrigued by the places we cannot visit, archetypal places that exist only in our psyche – such as hell, or paradise, or home. I'm curious how we define and signify these false utopias in the things we make, collect, and with which we surround ourselves, and in so doing, how we create idealised environments. Ceramics, with its long history of providing objects for eating, drinking, and other necessary rites, provokes my interest in intensifying the relationship between user and object. That this is a sensual relationship is emphasised by the sexual dimension of my forms. I want these objects to suggest a landscape of certain tactile pleasures and function as 'props' for an uneasy seduction. With this physical interaction, I recognise my work's potential to trigger memory, allow for character or role play, and create an interior landscape, a stage where things could happen.

Kim Dickey

Natasha Patkovski (Australia)

Fingerprint, h. 41 cm (16 in.), w. 15 cm (6 in.), 1999.

Surface: Fingerprint stamped clay slabs, pinched and joined construction. High-fired stoneware, oxidation.

This piece was constructed using a porcellaneous stoneware clay, joining up small pinched segments slabs, each impressed with a fingerprint stamp in the form of small clay rollers. The piece was constructed free-form, without the use of supporting moulds. Once bisqued, it was spray-glazed several times, with drying time between spraying, using a barium dry glaze for a textural, rough and dry-aged effect. The piece was fired in oxidation to 1300°C (2372°F).

Photograph: Terence Bogue

My work represents the fragility of identity spawned from the progressively decaying structural monuments of centuries past. At the same time it also reflects the strength on which these structures, civilisations, identities were based. My interest evolved from there to include current Australian multicultural society and notions of identity, whether they be personal, national or international. Perception has its limits that we unconsciously or consciously impose on ourselves, combined with those that are imposed on us by external agents. Identity is unique to the individual, as is the fingerprint. It is something you can see and touch, a visual link that distinguishes you from others. For many it is also the tool to unlocking your future, your path of life, destiny ever changing. The fingerprint may be seen as analogous to the labyrinth. It becomes a mark that reaffirms notions of personal identity.

Natasha Patkovski

Veronika Pöschl
(Netherlands) OPPOSITE PAGE

Stoneware Form, d. 37 cm (14 ½ in.), 1999.

Surface: Unglazed coil-built stoneware form. High-fired, reduction.

This form was meticulously and slowly constructed of uniform stoneware coils, each slightly stiffened before the next was put into place. Careful scraping inside joins the surface, while fine-line coil patterns remain on the outside. Work on one piece can take up to several weeks. The vessel was gas fired to 1250°C (2282°F) to promote varied and delicate surface tints.

Photograph: Johan van der Veer

In the powerful expression of archaic cultures I recognised an essential beauty. Plasticity, the specific characteristic of clay underlies all my ideas of volume, space, curved lines, round movement . . . therein the traditional vessel shape became my starting point and limit. As my work developed towards pure form any added decoration lost its meaning. Instead I discovered the natural signature of the skin which emerges during the work process. In the simple fingerwork of handbuilding I find the most direct and homogeneous expression of form and surface, inside and outside.

Veronika Pöschl

Madola (Spain)

Estel-La 94, h. 90 cm (35 ½ in.), w. 40 cm (15 ¾ in.), 1994.

Surface: Solid-block refractory clay construction with applied oxides and matt glazes. High-fired, oxidation.

This monumental piece was constructed of large blocks of cut refractory clay, assembled in three sections. After bisquing, the blocks were loosely painted and stained with metallic oxides and a matt cobalt glaze, and slowly electric fired to 1300°C (2372°F).

Photograph: Madola

Collection of Premià de Dalt

This work is part of a study of monolithic pillar forms, an exploration of ancient architectural 'memory constructions'. I seek to communicate a profound respect for the idea of memorial funeral works, capable of celebrating life and death, using clay as a lasting material that yet exhibits all marks of its creation, its passage through time. I aim for an absence of beauty in the literal sense, and more for an evocation of architectural permanence.

Madola

Bruce Cochrane (Canada)

Covered Jar, h. 28 cm (11 in.), w. 20 cm (8 in.), 2000.

Surface: Thrown, cut and reconstructed stoneware with fluting. High-fired, reduction.

The basic jar form was thrown upside down and bottomless, allowing for a heavily formed rim. Once leatherhard the conical form was inverted, squared off with a paddle and a bottom slab applied. Four thrown feet were attached to the corners of the base. Using a template, the rim was cut to accommodate a sloped roof-like lid constructed from a thrown and stretched disc of clay, fluted with a metal rib and formed over a plaster support. The spine or handle on the lid was also a thrown element. Once assembled the body was redefined with a grater-type tool known as a Surform, leaving a surface texture. This particular jar was made from stoneware clay, bisque fired, sprayed with a flashing slip and dipped in a black glaze to accent areas of the form. It was gas fired to 1250°C (2282°F) in a sodium vapour atmosphere.

Photograph: Peter Hogan
Courtesy of Prime Gallery, Toronto

After 25 years of working in clay, utility continues to serve as the foundation for my ideas. The potter's wheel has provided an immediacy and physicality in its process, which ideally supports these ideas about form and function. The pots I make, no matter how simple or complex, are meant to be experienced on a physical and visual level. The way an object carries, lifts, cradles, pours and contains are properties that I strive to make engaging for the user. Useful pottery, and its intimate connection with the daily rituals of life, has the potential for rich aesthetic experience.

Bruce Cochrane

Ruthanne Tudball (United Kingdom) OPPOSITE

Teapot on Three Feet, h. 45 cm (17 ¾ in.), 2000.

Surface: Wheel-thrown and wet-faceted, manipulated and assembled. High-fired stoneware, soda-glazed, reduction.

This teapot was wheel-thrown using stoneware, and manipulated and assembled on the wheel while wet. Faceting was done with a wirecutter on the slowly turning wheel, to capture the plasticity and fluidity of the clay. The piece was once-fired to 1300°C (2372°F), with bicarbonate of soda sprayed in solution into the kiln at 1260°C (4280°F) for about 2 ½ hours, at 15 minute intervals. At 950°C (1742°F), a light reduction took place, with another deliberate oxidation for the last 1 ½ hours of the firing.

Photograph: Ruthanne Tudball

I would like my pots to look as if they are still being thrown – are still evolving when they are finished. I draw my inspiration from the human body, as well as from the rhythmical movement in the earth: organic forms, tide, water and rock patterns, which are outward and visible signs of the movement, change and evolution that is going on around us all of the time. Sodium glazing is ideal for these forms because it can have dramatic effects on the surface of the pots. The sodium picks out every mark and emphasises the making process.

Ruthanne Tudball

Karen Koblitz
(United States)

My Obsession Series No.3 (detail),
h. 51 cm (20 in.), w. 20 cm (8 in.), 1999.

Surface: Low-relief carving, underglaze colours and transparent glaze. Low-fired earthenware, oxidation.

This tall vase form was thrown from white earthenware clay, and carved in low relief in the leatherhard stage. Coloured underglazes were brushed onto the greenware, and after bisquing to 1050°C (1922°F), the piece was coated with commercial transparent glaze and electric fired to 990°C (1814°F).

Photograph: Susan Einstein

There is a strong Italian influence to my work. I lived in Florence for one year where I studied the Renaissance works of the Della Robbia family. The most recent works in My Obsession Series *are based on a collectible passion that is irrational and has overcome my life. Here I am, schooled in the arts, and I have this fixation on buying small furry stuffed animals. I have taken this infatuation and integrated it into my artwork, elevating pop culture to the high-end decorative arts. My key influences in the art world are those painters involved with colour and pattern such as Henri Matisse, Edouard Vuillard, Miriam Shapiro, and Gustav Klimt. Teachers that have influenced my work are Viola Frey, Don Reitz and Bruce Breckenridge. In my work I pay homage to the functional roots of ceramics while elaborating on historical and decorative elements.*

Karen Koblitz

Susan Beiner (United States)

The Harvest Teapot, h. 25.5 cm (10 in.), w. 28 cm (11 in.), 2000.

Surface: Slipcast parts-encrusted surface. High-fired porcelain, oxidation.

After initial sketching out of ideas on paper, prototypes for cast parts (made out of clay or cast from found objects) were carefully and systematically 'glued' with slip onto a basic cast porcelain shape over a number of days. After careful drying and bisquing, coloured glazes were applied in successive layers, over repeated firings (up to four or five) down the temperature scale, from 1000°C (1832°F) to a final lustre firing at 700°C (1292°F).

Photograph: Susan Einstein

The Harvest Teapot tells the story of moving across the country to begin a new chapter of my life. It references the anxiety of being separated from my home and possessions, which are mostly a collection of objects that furnish me with emotional comfort. These objects become parts of the teapot: they are metaphors for my memories. The colours refer to a fall (autumn) harvest, symbolic of a new cycle of growth. I am obsessed with the energy of colour and the tactility of objects. This has led to mouldmaking, which in turn led to slipcasting. I am inspired by history, and how it relates to my current environment, appropriating the past into the present. In particular, I have been influenced by 17th- and 18th-century porcelain manufactures of Sèvres and Meissen, as well as engraved and cast surfaces of 18th-century Rococo domestic silverware.

Susan Beiner

Evelyn Klam (Germany)

Vessel, h. 30 cm (11 ¾ in.), 1999.

Surface: Press-moulded and thrown segment additions and sgraffito. Slabbed stoneware, mid-firing range, oxidation.

The vessel shape was built of slabbed, lightly-grogged stoneware, press-moulded over a plaster form. Handbuilt slab additions complete the shape and its base, and hand-formed as well as thrown-segment sections embellish the surface. In the leatherhard state, sgraffito patterning was added, along with coloured porcelain slips, and rubbed-in dark stains to accentuate the textural surface. The piece was covered with a wiped-down tin glaze and fired in oxidation to 1160°C (2120°F). Gold and platinum lustre details were added, and it was fired again to 750°C (1382°F).

Photograph: Gerald Zörner

I live in a part of Berlin that is very multicultural, and I am surrounded by visible Arab-oriental design elements that often inspire my own design sensibilities, cropping up as decorative elements: gold and silver, in the shapes of stars, flames and ornamental spheres. Although most of my pieces provide a smooth functional interior, I aim for a wildly playful, often rough external surface – a functional piece becomes ornate, celebratory and ceremonial.

Evelyn Klam

Jeannie Mah (Canada)

Cup with Sèvres Cup I, h. 28 cm (11 in.), w. 19 cm (7 ½ in.), 2000.

Surface: Clay cut-out, underglaze colour. High-fired porcelain, oxidation.

This piece was made of thin slab-built porcelain, rolled out on birch veneer, cut with an exacto knife, and formed around tissue paper. Commercial underglazes were applied in many layers like watercolours to the bisque surface, one colour applied per day to one side of the pot, to allow for water absorption on such a thin surface. Some areas were lightly rubbed away to expose the clay. A light wash of commercial opaque underglaze, high-fired and fluxed at 1300°C (2372°F), imparts a shimmer-like sheen to the surface, and often 'fights' with the underglaze coating beneath, to create an added distortion of the shape.

Photograph: Edward Jones
Courtesy of Prime Gallery, Toronto

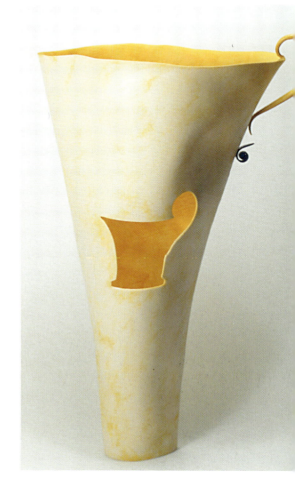

The history of ceramics and the translucency of porcelain is the subject of my research. I examine a history which is always in transition, yet often self-referential, and a materiality which is 'almost not there'. Ideas migrate by way of material culture, and I work from a reflection and a deflection of the ideas and ideals held within historical objects. I try to fold layers of our cultural influences into a single object, so as to reveal the underlying histories. I parody as I pay homage, which suggests an aesthetic movement in two directions at once. My research into porcelain examines form as it oscillates between movement and stability, and surface at the moment where the boundary between clay and glaze disappears.'

Jeannie Mah

Christine Thacker (New Zealand)

Cross Disc, d. 40 cm (15 ¾ in.), 1999.

Surface: Pierced and cut clay. Low-fired earthenware, oxidation.

The clay in this piece, containing a high ratio of grog and firebrick, was compacted into a former-mould, constructed of linoleum strips stapled around a baseboard. The soft clay was carved with metal-edged tools, and pierced extensively at the soft and leatherhard stages. After a slow bisque firing (20–25 hours), oxides and slips were applied for colour and texture, and several more low electric firings took place, between 1100°C (2012°F) and 1050°C (1922°F).

Photograph: Christine Thacker

I believe that everything you make contains everything you have ever made, every aesthetic you have embraced and all you have rejected, all that you have learned and all you have forgotten. Inspiration for me is from all sources and all experiences, and is received and expressed consciously and unconsciously. I have found inspiration in all forms: the body, the landscape, all aspects of nature and architecture everywhere. Currently I am inspired by simple geometry and using light as a material to be perceived as form. From contemporary ceramic history the works of Hans Coper are inspirational to me.

Christine Thacker

Gustavo Perez (Mexico) OPPOSITE

Vase, h. 36 cm (14 ¼ in.), w. 26 cm (10 ¼ in.), 2000.

Surface: Incised and distorted clay wall. High-fired stoneware, reduction.

This vase form was wheel-thrown from a self-mixed recipe of stoneware, and lightly 'sketched' over the outside with a fine blade, but not deep enough to pierce the clay wall. A careful distortion pushing out from the inside opened some of the fissures in a calculated way. Small beads of clay pressed in from the outside give the pattern continuity and rhythm. Once bisqued, the inside of the piece was glazed by pouring with a dark feldspathic glaze, and the outside was glazed by brush. The excess was then wiped off to leave only the slits glazed. The vase was gas fired in reduction to 1300°C (2372°F).

Photograph: Anthony Cuñha
Courtesy of Garth Clark Gallery, New York

I believe in work, in the unavoidable need an artist faces to make something very specific but ultimately impossible to understand fully; a sort of fate more than a decision or a choice. For me it is clay. Into this relation with clay should go somehow everything I care for: poetry, literature in general, music (from Monteverdi to music of our day), geometry, knots, maps, astronomical charts, curved mirrors, crystals, languages, the work of hundreds of artists (some ceramicists among them), labyrinths, the game of chess, seeds, and a long etcetera that would take pages to list and would certainly leave aside many things, probably the most important ones. Our memory keeps every single experience and processes it, in a conscious and unconscious way to produce what we can. In this impulse towards the Ithaca one would like to reach, lies for me the secret of creativity, trying endlessly to expose our intentions.

Gustavo Perez

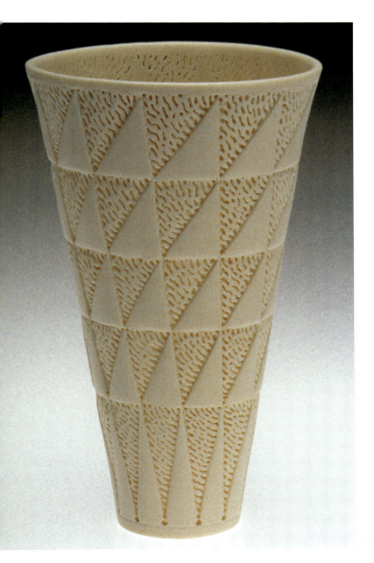

Sandra Black (Australia)

Tall Triangular Pierced Vessel, h. 16.5 cm (6 ½ in.), w. 9.5 cm (3 ¾ in.), 1999.

Surface: Low-relief carved and pierced polished porcelain. High-fired, oxidation.

This vessel was slipcast from a one-piece drop-out plaster mould, itself made from a solid wheel-thrown clay shape. Once removed from the mould, the thin-walled vessel was slightly trimmed, and horizontal banded lines established for the pattern with a surgical blade. After low-relief carving, the fine holes were drilled with a Dremel drill and fine dental bit, the piece was carefully sanded and dusted when dry and, after bisquing, soaked and wet-polished. After an electric firing to 1220°C (2228°F), it was wet- and dry-polished again to a smooth, silky surface.

Photograph: Victor France
Courtesy of Viscopy (Image Rights), Australia

Porcelain for me is the most seductive of all the clays. While difficult to work with, its whiteness, translucency, density and surface more than compensate for any problems. Thematically, I pursue the simplest possible forms to carry my elaborate surface decorations and to express my interest in geometry and division of space.

Sandra Black

Mary Roehm (United States)

Punctuated Bowl, h. 45.7 cm (18 in.), w. 66 cm (26 in.), 2000.

Surface: Punctured thrown and altered porcelain. High-fired, reduction.

This flared porcelain bowl was wheel-thrown, altered and punctured while still wet, to the point of challenging the structural integrity of the form. After drying, the piece was wood fired in a downdraught catenary arch kiln to 1320°C (2408°F), at which point the porcelain begins to move and soften. Subtle colour variations occur through flashing and ash deposits.

Photograph: Storm Photo

The vessel has a rich history and meaning in the craft tradition and provides ample opportunity for my investigation and personal interpretation. The materials and processes I work with have their own histories that I elect to contradict. Porcelain brings to mind images of highly refined, classical forms. As I became adept working with porcelain, it became increasingly easy to push the boundaries of the material. I work to create a tension between the viewer's visceral and intellectual reactions. Working with porcelain and throwing in particular, is drawing three-dimensionally. The quality and weight of the drawn line conveys unconscious meaning and with porcelain, fully reveals the individual.

Mary Roehm

Sidsel Hanum (Norway)

Black Night, h. 14 cm (5 ½ in.), w. 19 cm (7 ½ in.), 1997.

Surface: Perforated porcelain from inside. High-fired, reduction.

This oval shape was thrown in two parts with Limoges porcelain and altered. Repeated perforations were made from inside by pressing a needle through the clay wall, in this case with a slightly downward drag, for an overall repeating pattern and a specific effect of light and shadow. After bisquing, thin layers of various coloured feldspathic glazes were double-dipped to give a velvety waterfall-like effect to the surface. The piece was oil fired in reduction to 1300°C (2372°F).

Photograph: Dannevig Foto

I see my work as minimalist and simple, relying more on rhythmic textural patterns than on overtly bright colours. Understated movement on the edge of walls of a piece create a quiet dance on forms that are simple variants of the basic cylinder. Shells, spikes, nails, stones and other found objects are continually gathered for eventual inclusion in some work. The contemplation of art and architecture during my travels provides an important stimulus to further creation.

Sidsel Hanum

Frank Boyden (United States)

Golden Fish Vase, h. 31.5 cm (12 ½ in.), 1999.

Surface: Clay distortion and clay sgraffito. High-fired porcelain, reduction.

This wheel-thrown vase was made of Limoges porcelain, distorted from inside while wet, to accommodate the external sgraffito fish pattern. The piece was sprayed with a saturated manganese glaze, and wood fired with alder and fir wood in an Anagama kiln over 2 ½ to 3 ½ days, to 1300–1350°C (2372°–2462°F). There was a heavy body reduction and a general oxidising fire towards the end of the firing cycle.

Photograph: Jim Piper

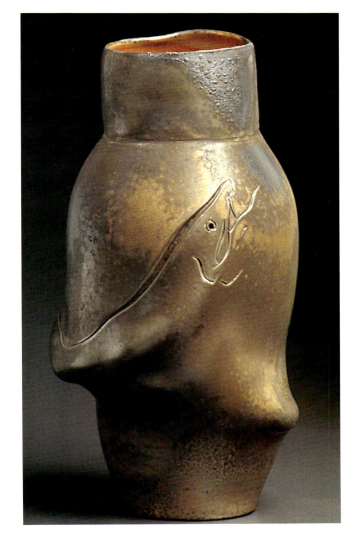

I live on the Oregon coast, where the elements have their way. I am surrounded by animals and big trees. My work is taken from this microcosm. I draw on everything and my clay surfaces and forms are made to draw on. I deform the tight porcelain surfaces to emphasise the incisions. Often they are pushed to the point of collapse and I am interested in the violence this implies. The delicacy and somewhat sacred quality of porcelain is pushed very far and often put into jeopardy. I am interested in ceramics of many cultures but I especially like the forms and drawing of the Mayas, the work from Ica and Paracas on the south Peruvian coast, Minoan and Mimbres pots, and the delicacy and dance of sculptural Korean Silla work.

Frank Boyden

Hans and Birgitte Börjeson (Denmark)

Bowl, d. 60 cm (23 ½ in.), 1998.

Surface: Stoneware with clay sgraffito, thin layered slip, once-fired. High-fired salt glaze, stoneware, reduction.

The initial bowl form made of light-coloured thrown stoneware, was slightly altered by hand from within. When leatherhard, fine line-drawing sgraffito was made, and the lines were filled with black stain. The grooves were then carefully closed with a hard tool, and surplus stain lightly washed away with a soft sponge, for an overall delicate etching effect. A thin solution of stain in a contrasting colour coated the background, then a thin coating of matt white slip was sprayed on. The piece was once-fired in a gas kiln, in reduction to 1300°C (2372°F), with several saltings, beginning at 1250°C (2282°F). Ordinary fine dry kitchen salt was sprayed into the kiln with a sandblasting gun.

Photograph: Ole Wolbye

We collaborate closely on almost every piece of work. Forms are organic and developed from impressions received on our travels in the Near and Far East, and from two years of working in Africa. The sgraffito technique, if used figuratively, is a very direct way to express ideas – much like African artists scratching stories on their calabashes, the ancient Greeks depicting their life stories on amphorae, or ancient peoples carving or painting their cave walls in Altamira. As modern craftspeople, we have the privilege of building on these traditions in our own way.

Hans and Birgitte Börjeson

Jack Doherty (United Kingdom)

Slab dish, 45 x 45 cm (17 ¾ x 17 ¾ in.), 1998.

Surface: Cut and incised clay surface. High-fired porcelain, reduction.

This slab plate was made using wooden formers and was loosely pattern-cut in the wet state. It was fired in a propane-fuelled kiln, with bicarbonate of soda and water injected with a pressurised garden sprayer for approximately two hours at 1260°C (2300°F). Final firing temperature was to 1300°C (2372°F).

Photograph: Jack Doherty

I make porcelain which explores and extends the qualities associated with this beautiful material. I make functional pots which range in scale from fine delicate cups for tea or cider to large unexpectedly rugged slab dishes and plates. The pots which we use every day can change how we see or feel about the food which we place in them. I put apples and plums into the dishes with care, enjoying their softness. I enjoy the way in which the soda glaze marks and articulates the surface of the forms with the trace of flame and vapour. It is a dramatic and exciting procedure which is the final creative act in my making process.

Jack Doherty

Coll Minogue
(Republic of Ireland)

Slab, 24 X 24 cm (9 ½ x 9 ½ in.), 1999.

Surface: Corrugated cardboard-impressed stoneware. High-fired, reduction.

This stoneware slab was wet-impressed with corrugated cardboard, with an added light kaolin/ball clay slip coating. The piece was once-fired in a wood kiln with a Bourry-type firebox, over 24–30 hours, to 1300°C (2372°F).

Photograph: John McKenzie

I became aware of the textures on the powerful pots from throughout history, particularly those from the Japanese Jomon period, Neolithic and Early Bronze Age in Britain and Ireland, the Early Cycladic Period and the Cypriot Bronze Age. I became more and more interested in how these marks were made and compared them to the mark-making techniques used by contemporary ceramic artists. When I began wood firing in the early 1980s the mark-making became less decorative, as I learned to appreciate and work with the fired effects it is possible to achieve. I began using found objects, particularly various grades of corrugated card, to create textures by impressing into soft slabs of clay. I wanted these impressions to be understated (rather than very obvious) so that they could be quietly accentuated by flame and fly ash during firing, while adding depth and interest to the clay surface.

Coll Minogue

Tom Turner (United States)

Lidded Jar, h. 45 cm (17 ¾ in.), w. 30 cm (11 ¾ in.), 2000.

Surface: Paddled textural surface. High-fired stoneware, reduction.

This large lidded jar was thrown with coils, and paddled for surface texture. After dippings into a turquoise ash glaze, some of the glaze was sponged off to reveal surface irregularities. The jar was fired in a natural gas kiln, with oxidation to 1000°C (1832°F), and a medium reduction to 1300°C (2372°F).

Photograph: Ken Van Dyne

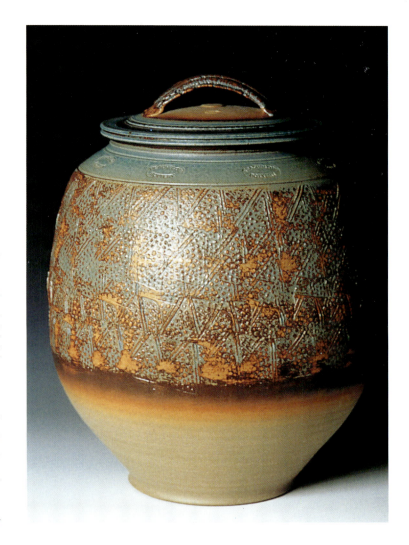

I am not a painter and try to avoid brushes as much as possible. I start with the strongest form I can throw, creating surface textures where possible and then using a glaze that is appropriate to the form and to the pot's surface. I purposely leave a lot of clay unglazed as I love the warmth of reduced stoneware. Currently, almost all of my pots are paddled to create surface texture, or to change the vertical shape of the pot to oval, triangular, or square. I like glazes that develop their character in the firing rather than relying on surface painting.

Tom Turner

Monika J. Schoedel-Müller (Germany)

Vessel, d. 30 cm (11 ¾ in.), 2000.

Surface: Sandblasted stoneware. High-fired black glaze, third-firing lustre, oxidation.

This vessel was made of thickly-thrown and trimmed white stoneware, whose surface was coarsely sandblasted in the leatherhard state. After bisquing, a black feldspathic glaze was sprayed on the piece and it was fired in oxidation to 1300°C (2372°F). The inner portion of the vessel was gold-lustred and the piece was refired to 800°C (1472°F).

Photograph: W.B. Nowka

Contrasts and visual differences are often an enticement to contemplation. In this instance the smooth inner gold surface, with its inherent language of preciousness, strongly contrasts with the rough, black rock- and lava-like outer surface. Disparity is deliberately created by two contrasting visual values.

Monika J. Schoedel-Müller

Peter Fraser Beard (United Kingdom)

Sail Form, h. 45 cm (17 ¾ in.), 1999.

Surface: Stamp-impressed stoneware surface. High-fired, oxidation.

This sail form was constructed of Molochite-grogged stoneware (T-material), built with semi-soft slabs and refined when leatherhard. The stamps (each one different) were made by pulling a stretched spring through wet clay, the separated and stiffened sections being cut up into the various stamp patterns, subsequently bisqued. A grid of small squares was marked into the leatherhard sail form surface, a touch of slurry was applied to each square, and the stamps were impressed, several hundred times. After bisquing, the object was washed with iron, manganese and copper, and fired in oxidation to 1300°C (2372°F).

Photograph: Peter Fraser Beard

The main objective of my work is to produce beautiful objects that are very contemporary, but nonetheless have an allegiance to history, giving them a timeless quality. Landscape in all forms is my main source of inspiration, along with the art of ancient Egypt.

Peter Fraser Beard

Kate Malone *(United Kingdom)*

Mother Teapot, h. 48 cm (19 in.), w. 92 cm (36 ¼ in.), 1998.

Surface: Sprig-decorated coil-construction with coloured crystalline glazes. High-fired stoneware, oxidation.

This enormous oval-shaped teapot was coil-constructed on an oval slab base, with added hollowed-out solid clay spout and knob components. A few plaster-moulded sprigs were applied in the leatherhard stage, with details modelled through thin plastic film (clingfilm/Saran wrap). After drying and bisquing, clear coloured high-alkaline crystalline glazes were applied by brush, and the teapot was fired to 1260°C (2300°F) in oxidation, with controlled cooling for crystal growth.

Photograph: Stephen Brayne

The teapot form is loosely based on a British traditional 'Brown Betty' teapot – the shape produced in Stoke-on-Trent in England, and used for decades by all classes of households. I did not really consciously plan this but have this form ingrained in my mind through familiarity. A teapot to me symbolises a time of realising and sharing – the fact that it is a large one is supposed to increase the effect. The surface of this big heavy woman of a form (a mother) is decorated with sprigs of crest or coat-of-arms type images which are also symbolic. A pumpkin for fecundity, a pineapple for prosperity, a pitcher for sharing, a gourd for fertility, a bee for industry, a necklace of leaves, and spout of daisies for Mother nature.

Kate Malone

Matthew Metz (United States) OPPOSITE

Jar, h. 15 cm (6 in.), 1997.

Surface: Applied sprigs on porcelain, salt-glazed. High-fired, oxidation.

This lidded jar was wheel-thrown and trimmed using porcelain, with surface sprigs added at the leatherhard stage. After bisquing, the piece was glazed with an interior liner glaze, and salt fired to 1300°C (2372°F) in a wood/oil kiln, in a neutral/oxidation atmosphere.

Photograph: Peter Lee

My functional pots add another dimension, I hope, to the user's everyday life. Influences are diverse, ranging from early American pots, quilts, and folk art, to Asian and European ceramic traditions. Though the images resist a specific narrative reading, the iconography has been chosen for its personal resonance.

Matthew Metz

Merilyn Wiseman (New Zealand)

Pacific Rim, 130 x 45 x 38 cm (51 x 17 ¾ x 15 in.), 1996.

Surface: Combed white earthenware with a copper high-magnesium glaze. Low-fired oxidation.

This form was initially constructed upside down, with two large triangular slabs of earthenware (strengthened with Molochite), folded around a curved oval former. The outside surface was combed, using a slightly concave comb cut from flexible linoleum. After bisquing, a copper high-magnesium glaze was sprayed on in varying thicknesses to cause light crawling and beading, revealing the contrasting clay surface. The piece was fired in oxidation to 1200°C (2192°F).

Photograph: Stephanie Leeves

Tools distance the artist's hands from most materials. But, for the potter, clay is real 'Hands-on stuff. Hands-in stuff!' I spent my New Zealand childhood in a land surrounded by ocean. Textures, felt through bare feet and curious hands, were those of sand, water, clay cliffs and coastal rock formations. In the search for new life in new forms I so often ask the question 'but what if…?' It is all a continuous process. I think of the Zen phrase 'It's much like riding the ox in search of the ox'.

Merilyn Wiseman

chapter two

Colour in clay

Colour in clay examines some of those techniques that deal specifically with the use of coloured clays to create integral surface patterns, without the use of masking coloured glazes. A translation from the Japanese of *nerikomi* and *neriage* suggest the techniques: 'neri', to mix and 'komi', to press into. Thus *nerikomi* is the technique of pressing coloured clays into a mould to create pattern, and *neriage* the technique of throwing layered coloured clays on the wheel, much like marbleised agateware. *Millefiori*, the Italian version of *nerikomi*, refers back to a similar technique in glassware. Other techniques in this chapter include clay mosaic, laminating (bonding layers of coloured clays), laminating and slicing, poured overlapping coloured slips, and *mishima* inlay (from the Korean), which involves filling incised patterns of clay with contrasting clays, and scraping the surface flush.

Renée Reichenbach (Germany)

Kasten mit Stacheltier (Box with Porcupine), 29 x 24 x 65 cm (11 ¼ x 9 ½ x 25 ½ in.), 1998.

Surface: Inlaid coloured clays with sgraffito and rubbed-in oxides, slip and glaze painting. Mid-range fired stoneware, oxidation.

This piece was handbuilt from grogged clay slabs, with varied patterning scraps of porcelain, white or dyed, rolled flat into their surface. The multicoloured slabs were then sgraffito-sketched over with a fine needle, then cut in the pre-leatherhard stage, and constructed into the given shape. After bisquing, surfaces were sanded smooth and sgraffito lines rubbed in with black stain for graphic accents. Some surface areas were touched up with porcelain slips, and transparent or white glazes were sprayed, poured and brushed on before a final oxidation firing to 1160°C (2120°F). Several firings may occur to promote the final desired effect.

Photograph: Reinhard Hentze

A new piece begins for me with the intensive study of the finished, rolled out slab. Guided by the 'colour-moments' of the slabs, I plan the new piece. I need these 'moments' to help my fantasy develop a consequent form. One might say they take away my fear of the 'white, unwritten page'. The original ideas for my pieces are almost always functional ones. When I have finally found a form that pleases me – be it a teapot, a vessel or a plate – I then view it as an abstraction. This frees me from all formal rules. I feel completely free to change, to add or take away, to complicate or simplify – a rich, sensual, and living experience for me. This leads me towards my ultimate goal: to mould the body and the surface (skin) of the piece into a rhythmic whole.

Renée Reichenbach

Mieke Everaet (Belgium)

Flower Fragments, Porcelain Bowl Form, d. 16 cm (6 ¼ in.), 2000.

Surface: Inlaid coloured porcelain mosaic. High-fired, oxidation.

A variety of coloured porcelain slips were created by additions of oxides and body stains to porcelain powder. Finely cut thin porcelain strips were systematically laid down inside a pre-determined vessel-shaped mould. Once leatherhard, the piece itself was carefully scraped down and the pattern emerged as the clay wall itself, identical inside and out. After long and careful drying, the piece was bisqued to 1000°C (1832°F) and after bisquing the bowl form was finely sanded and then high-fired in oxidation to 1300°C (2372°F) in sand moulds to avoid deformation. Afterwards, a final polish with very fine water sandpaper gave a silky overall patina.

Photograph: Hans Vos

One source of inspiration for my mosaic-inlay bowl shapes was an exhibition of Renaissance Venetian agate dinnerware, where the stone itself was the pattern, an organic blend of line, colour and transparency. The forms of nature also provide standards for proportion and harmony, in regard to the growing process and the coherence of form, colour, and pattern that one can observe in the inherent geometry of Nature.

Mieke Everaet

Hanna Schneider (Switzerland)

Two Bowls, d. 16 cm (6 ¼ in.), d. 14 cm (5 ½ in.), 1996.

Surface: *Neriage*-type decoration, wheel-thrown coloured clays. Low-fired stoneware, oxidation.

These bowls were made using a light Limoges stoneware body, with a 20% addition of gerstley borate to encourage colour brilliance and promote low-fire vitrification. Clays were coloured using copper carbonate, chrome oxide, cobalt carbonate and red iron oxide. Varying colours and thicknesses of clay were compressed together, thrown on the wheel, trimmed when leatherhard, slowly dried, and finely polished with steel wool. The pieces were fired in oxidation to 950°C (1742°F).

Photograph: Hugo Jeger

I have long had an interest in the diversity of both texture and colour inherent in clays. There is a fascination and satisfaction in the shaping and patterning of a vessel occurring simultaneously without the need for a separate glazing process. Various sojourns in Mexico, and staying with potters there, observing their skilful handing of clay, no doubt influenced my own approach to working.

Hanna Schneider

Jane Waller (United Kingdom)

Reflective Bowl, h. 11 cm (4 ¼ in.), w. 21.5 cm (8 ½ in.), 1994.

Surface: Pestled inlaid *millefiori* coloured clays. Low-fired, oxidation.

This bowl was made from oxide-stained coloured earthenware clays, carefully pestled inside a thick self-made plaster mould. The thickness of the mould allows for the pestling movement which spreads and joins the coloured clays. These were of varying moisture contents, drier clay promoting straighter lines, moist clay more curved patterns. After scraping, compressing and careful drying over three weeks, the bowl was bisqued and glazed with a semi-matt transparent glaze, and fired to 1100°C (2012°F) in oxidation, followed by a fine sandblasting.

Photograph: Jane Waller

I create ceramics where decoration is integrated with form. The inspiration for this new method came from blowing goblets during my MA course in Ceramics and Glass at the Royal College of Art. In millefiori glass, colours are stretched and altered within the glass walls both by expansion (from air) and by movement (from manipulating the blowpipe). I decided to transfer this to ceramics, so that the patterns could go right through the clay walls.

Jane Waller

Curtis Benzle (United States)

Patchwork, h. 20 cm (8 in.), w. 48 cm (19 in.), 1998.

Surface: *Nerikomi* (*millefiori*) coloured clay inlays with slips. High-fired porcelain, oxidation.

This shape was constructed from two porcelain panels. *Nerikomi* rolls of coloured clays were sliced endwise across the grain to reveal the pattern, and laid out collage-style into panels. These were flipped over, painted with graduated slip on the back, flipped back, and white slip painted between pattern joints, with added black dot slip inlay. The panels were rolled flat, and laid and joined in a specially created saggar of castable refractory. After drying and bisquing, the piece was sanded, fired in oxidation to 1260°C (2300°F), and fine-sanded again.

Photograph: Curtis Benzle

My involvement with coloured porcelain has been a purposeful evolution – an exploration of technique in search of the means to unlock an ideal of beauty. The essence of this aesthetic ideal is most readily evidenced when light is filtered through space. An early morning mist that partially obscures meadows and trees; a swirling eddy, capable of concealing from clear sight the fish within; or an eggshell-thin porcelain bowl, able to capture light and heighten our awareness of passing rays. When light combines with the fineness of porcelain, I feel I possess the means and material required to pursue my aesthetic mission.

Curtis Benzle

Thomas Hoadley (United States)

Untitled Vessel, h. 25.5 cm (10 in.), 2000.

Surface: Sliced and assembled coloured porcelain clays. High-fired, oxidation.

This vessel was constructed using the *nerikomi* technique. Stain-dyed porcelain clays were sliced and stacked in various ways to create blocks of patterned clays. Cross-sectional slices from various blocks were joined to each other and added to a drape-moulded bowl base. The completed form was compressed, stretched into its final shape, and carefully scraped down, inside and out, when leatherhard. After sanding and bisquing, the piece was wet-sanded, fired in oxidation to 1180°C (2156°F), wet-sanded again, and finally sealed with a water seal, followed by a rubbed-off coating of mineral oil.

Photograph: Thomas Hoadley

My current ceramic work reflects several areas of interest. One is in the vessel as an abstract sculptural form and its many associations, both literal and metaphoric. Another is pattern and colour and how a collection of abstract elements can create various feelings or impressions. A third is an interest in the integration of surface pattern and three-dimensional form. The penetration of the pattern through the thickness of the wall so as to be visible on both the outside and the inside, is a partial solution to the problem; but from a strictly two-dimensional standpoint I am also concerned with how the pattern relates to the form as seen in profile.

Thomas Hoadley

Clare Rutter (United Kingdom)

Katy Blue Bowl, h. 5 cm (2 in.), w. 11 cm (4 ¼ in.), 1997.

Surface: Laminated layers of coloured clay, cut and reassembled. High-fired porcelain, oxidation.

Fine slabs of laminated coloured clays were cut into pattern shapes and pressed into a plate-mould bowl form. After bisquing, no glaze was applied and the piece was refired to 1230°C (2246°F). This almost translucent thin porcelain bowl displays the same pattern inside and outside, in the clay wall itself.

Photograph: Dick Hodgkinson

My work is fuelled by fictional worlds inspired by marine life and insects, both supplying an abundance of colours and forms. The pieces I produce explore the ritual and ceremonial events of these worlds. In the case of insects the more I researched them the more I became fascinated by the similarities between their rituals and those of humans. For example the giving of gifts for sexual favours; this inspired a series of platters, as many of the gifts were food. Also the brilliance of colour of male insects when in pursuit of a mate in comparison to the brilliance of human tribal decoration used for the same purpose.

Clare Rutter

Dorothy Feibleman (United Kingdom)

Coral Lunar, h. 12.5 cm (5 in.), w. 23 cm (9 in.), 1999.

Surface: Colour-saturated Parian paste, cut and laminated. Low-fired, oxidation.

In this open vessel shape, rolls of cut and laminated, colour saturated Parian soft paste were assembled flat, then pressed into a bisque form. After drying and bisquing to 900°C (1652°F), the piece was fine-sanded and refired in oxidation to 1120°C (2048°F). The darker oxide colours expand more during firing, adding subtle qualities of shape distortion. The yellow to coral colours were created by colour weight addition to the initial paste, in up to 166 gradations of colour.

Photograph: Mark Johnston

The title of this piece comes from my perception of it as something foreign or otherworldly. Perhaps, if visiting another planet, this is how an organic shape might manifest itself. Although I can anticipate effects of colour and shape, this piece emerged with exceptional clarity, surpassing my expectations, affirming both research and procedures.

Dorothy Feibleman

Dorothy Feibleman (United Kingdom)

Window to Atlantis, h. 17 cm (6 ¾ in.), w. 17 cm (6 ¾ in.), 1995–2000.

Surface: Laminated varying temperature off-white clays. High-fired Parian paste and porcelain, oxidation.

This piece was constructed of varying kinds of porcelains and Parian paste carefully saved and kept over a few years. Groupings of pattern comprising various rolled, cut and laminated clays were assembled flat, pressed into a bisque mould, dried slowly, and scraped smooth with a metal rib and double-edged curved razor. After being electric fired to 900°C (1652°F) and 1120°C (2048°F), with intermittent sanding, the piece was refired to 1230°C (2246°F), and finely sanded with fine diamond paper. The inclusion of lower-maturing Parian clay, held into the structure by the higher-fired porcelain, promotes varied subtle colour and translucency effects.

Photograph: Mark Johnston

I consider Window to Atlantis *to be a reflection of my search for hidden qualities, revealed by light, like a treasure found underwater, or the mystery of certain kinds of light seen in Venetian patterning. With tools and process becoming an extension of myself, I hope for some clarity and am delighted when materials and process engender their own surprises and mystery.*

Dorothy Feibleman

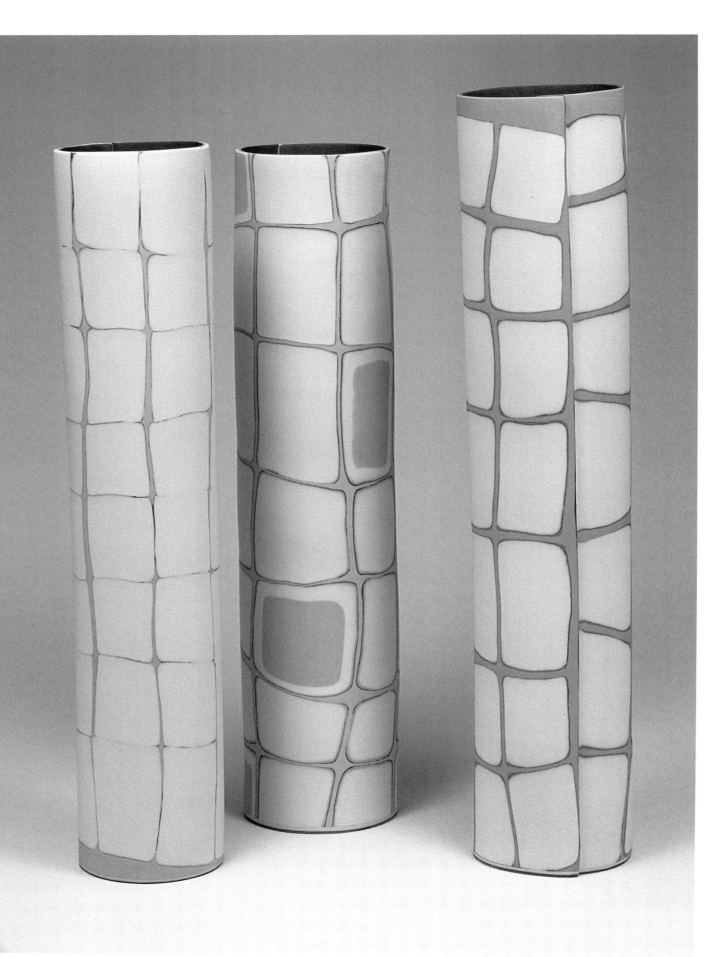

Sasha Wardell
(United Kingdom)

Incised Vase, h. 22 cm (8 ¾ in.), 1998;
Sliced Bowl, h. 11 cm (4 ¼ in.), 1999–2000.

Surface: Laminated layers of incised and sliced coloured bone china. High-fired, oxidation.

These pieces were slipcast in self-made moulds, using coloured liquid bone china, poured successively in and out of the moulds in several colour coat layers that remained laminated together. After deliberate distortion in the leatherhard stage, the pieces were dried and pared down in patterns with a sharp blade to reveal the different colour layers. They were soft-fired to 1000°C (1832°F), sanded and refired in oxidation to 1260°C (2300°F). A final wet polishing occurred, using fine emery paper, to create an eggshell-type finish.

Photograph: Mark Lawrence

Bone china, with all its idiosyncrasies, has remained my favourite material. It is a very 'single-minded' clay which forces clarity and precision whilst demanding perseverance. Possessing qualities of intense whiteness, translucency and strength, it is a very seductive material to work with, although its inflexibility and restrictive nature can limit and discourage at times. Architectural detail and sections of structures, combined with an interest in illusions provide the starting point for the pieces whilst the inherent qualities of the clay do the rest – its whiteness offers a pure blank canvas for the application of colour and its translucency enhances any varying degrees of luminosity.

Sasha Wardell

Susan Nemeth (United Kingdom) OPPOSITE

Three Porcelain Vases, h. 35 cm (13 ¾ in.), 2001.

Surface: Inlaid laminated coloured porcelain. High-fired, oxidation.

These cylinders were made of slab-constructed porcelain. All patterning was done while the slabs were laid out flat, before construction. A black sheet of clay was rolled out, covered by a laminated sheet of coloured porcelain. After a coating of black slip, contrasting inlaid clays were rolled in to make the pattern, and the remaining black slip was washed off to leave a dark outline around the inlays. After construction, the pieces were low-fired and polished, and embedded in sand-filled saggars to prevent warping in the final firing to 1300°C (2372°F).

Photograph: Stephen Brayne

I am currently influenced by 1950s and 1960s fabric designs. I also look at painters such as Ben Nicholson and Paul Klee, and am influenced by their simplicity and understanding of colour. In the past I have also looked at Matisse and Sonia Delaunay. The technique of using layers of coloured clays and slip started for me when I was at college from 1975–78. I was surrounded by derelict houses with layers of peeling wallpaper and was fascinated by the revealing layers. I like the quality of unglazed porcelain, stained to achieve soft, subtle colours. I also like the fact that the design is integral, so it stretches to fit the shape when moulded.

Susan Nemeth

Zenji Miyashita
(Japan)

Spout of Wind, h. 47 cm (18 ½ in.),
w. 38 cm (15 in.), 2000.

Surface: Poured overlapping polychrome slips. High-fired porcelain, reduction.

This shape was constructed using thick paper cut-out templates to create porcelain slabs. Several hours later, the supporting paper was removed from the joined slabs, and progressive layers of coloured slips were poured over. Porcelain slip was dyed with such oxides as cobalt, manganese, chrome, nickel and titanium to create a subtle palette of over 100 colours. After bisquing, the piece was thinly sprayed with a colourless clear glaze and gas fired in reduction to 1250°C (2282°F).

Photograph: T. Hatakeyama

I place emphasis on poetically depicting landscapes as I picture them in my mind, by using coloured clay rather than painting on beautiful landscapes as they are. In the course of one's life one experiences various occurrences, some of which are moving or blissful and others puzzling or afflictive. Natural scenes such as a striking morning scene full of sunlight and a melancholy but picturesque twilight, remind one of such occurrences. I would like to translate mental images of such landscapes deeply impressed on my mind into ceramic works which make those who see them respond to the wishes and feelings expressed in them, such as joy, sorrow and peace of mind.

Zenji Miyashita

Jeannie van der Putten
(New Zealand)

Safe Harbour, 90 x 75 cm (35 ½ x 29 ½ in.) 1999.

Surface: *Mishima* clay inlay. Mid-firing range, earthenware clays, oxidation.

This set of 'tiles' for the wall was made of hand-sized pieces of hand-cut terracotta clay, incised and inlaid at the leatherhard stage with white clay and scraped down. The birds were lightly burnished with a spoon and sponge, the star form was left grogged and rough, and flower forms were bisqued and glazed in copper green and iron yellow. The pieces were electric fired to 1160°C (2120°F).

Photograph: Haru Sameshima

The wall installation Safe Harbour *reflects Auckland with its large Polynesian population, the Haraki Gulf with the volcanic island of Rangitoto, and the wider Pacific basin. Hibiscus, frangipani, palm, bird and star forms (notably the Southern Cross) all form a sort of ceramic 'tapa' cloth for the wall. Indigenous crafts, such as incising and carving of wood and gourds, mother-of-pearl inlay, and weaving, have all contributed to my work in clay.*

Jeannie van der Putten

chapter three
Dry-surface decoration

Dry-surface decoration in the context of this book refers to a ceramic surface with deliberate non-use of glaze – with the exception of those unglazed surfaces that rely more on firing effects (i.e. ash deposits, vapour-glazing, flashing marks, etc.), which are more specifically examined in Chapter Nine (Fire, Smoke and Ash Surfaces). Dry-surface decoration in this chapter includes the use of stains and oxides, dry slips, air-brushing techniques, terra sigillata, vitreous engobes, slip sgraffito and carving, slip inlay, and layered slips with wiped-down glazes. All types of clays, firing methods and temperatures may be included here.

Clare Conrad (United Kingdom)

Vessel, h. 23 cm (9 in.), 1999.

Surface: Cloth-applied layered, coloured vitreous slips. High-fired stoneware, oxidation.

This vessel was thrown and trimmed using a smooth stoneware blended with T-material (a specially formulated high-Molochite clay that can be thinly stretched, with minimum warpage and shrinkage). Once leatherhard, various layers of carefully-graded coloured vitreous slips were applied by layering with cloths, taking care to maintain awareness of ratio of dampness of slip to the pot itself. After bisquing, the interior was glazed with a colour-harmonised satin matt glaze, and the piece was fired in oxidation to 1200°C (2192°F).

Photograph: Clare Conrad

My work encompasses and consolidates long-term interests in art and archaeology, expressed through sculptural container forms. My approach is to combine artistic expression with traditional craft skills and an innovative decorating technique – an on-going exploration of texture and colour. Form and contrast were my initial concerns, with particular interest in contradictions such as fragile strength and rugged delicacy, and aesthetic obsessions with chiaroscuro and visual drama. The sun-baked colours and sense of mellow antiquity experienced in the Mediterranean provided the stimulus for experiments with colour and texture. Other diverse influences include ancient Egyptian pottery, prehistoric implements, paintings by Mark Rothko, Modigliani and Jacob van Ruisdael, combined with the smoke flashings of wood-fired ceramics. I aim for elegant, atmospheric, contemplative pots that are strongly contemporary, whilst showing references to the past.

Clare Conrad

Jeroen Bechthold
(Netherlands)

Requiem for 6 Dead Animals,
h. 37 cm (14 ½ in.), w. 52 cm (20 ¼ in.), 1995.

Surface: Stain-impressed and painted porcelain slabs with sprig additions. High-fired, oxidation.

This piece was constructed of thin porcelain slabs, assembled into a loose organic structure. Oxides and stains were rolled into the initial porcelain slabs with added painted accent details. Low-relief sprigs provide a textural element and encourage the pooling of oxide colours. Once bisqued, the piece was gas fired in oxidation to 1240°C (2264°F), having been glazed on the inside with a thick glaze and later coated with 22-carat gold lustre. The outer surface remains dry, with colour and texture more reminiscent of a natural rock surface.

Photograph: Anita de Jong

During a period of very isolated work in Jordan in 1995, I adopted a family of cats that subsequently died, one by one. This piece is a symbiosis, if you like, of the examination of such diverse elements as the grief at losing pets, the frustration with lost work, as well as the powerful impressions imprinted upon me by the beauty of the amazing rock formations at Petra in Jordan. Work can be both nostalgic and commemorative, healing, and a catharsis of past grief, allowing one to move on.

Jeroen Bechthold

Peter Lane (United Kingdom)

Evening Sky, w. 30 cm (11 ¾ in.), 1999.

Surface: Freehand underglaze colour airbrush painting. High-fired porcelain, oxidation.

This thrown and trimmed porcelain bowl, after bisquing, was carefully sanded and all surface dust was removed. Underglaze colours and stains were mixed together and passed through a 200s mesh cup sieve before use. The graded colours were airbrushed freehand, with careful cleaning with water between sprayings to avoid uncontrolled splatters of pigment due to blockages in the airbrush. A final oxidising firing took place at 1260–1300°C (2300–2372°F), and the bowl was finally polished with wet-and-dry silicon carbide paper.

Photograph: Peter Lane

Porcelain, with its fine texture, purity and whiteness, allows me to explore relationships between form and surface in a way that is more rewarding than with any other clay. Wheel-thrown vessel forms offer infinite opportunities for subtle variations, but my particular concern, while attempting to achieve harmony and balance in the work, is to express my feelings for the natural world through the positive radiation of light and colour. Skies, sea and landscapes, together with the multitude of flora, are a constant source of wonder, inspiration and delight to me.

Peter Lane

Werner B. Nowka (Germany)

Two Body Forms, h. 70 cm (27 ½ in.), 1998.

Surface: Air-brushed black and white slips on rib-surfaced stoneware. High-fired, oxidation.

The two shapes here were slab-constructed of white stoneware with rib-shaped manipulations made in the soft leatherhard state. When dry, the forms were carefully air-brushed with a fine-nozzle spray gun with black and white slips to reinforce the three-dimensionality of the surface. After bisquing, a black feldspathic glaze covered the interiors, and black slip touching-up of the rim occurred. The pieces were electric fired in oxidation to 1300°C (2372°F).

Photograph: Werner B. Nowka

My objective here is to confuse and intrigue viewers, to repeatedly engage them in the questioning of an illusory surface. What is form, what is painting? Is it body or vessel, two-dimensional surface, or three-dimensional sculpture? The ceramic medium is ideal for engendering such confusions, such questions, such dialogue.

Werner B. Nowka

Misun Rheem (South Korea)

Through the Flower I, d. 20.5 cm (8 in.), 1998.

Surface: Thickly applied dry slip. High-fired porcelain, oxidation.

This shape was coil-constructed over a clay slab pressed onto a plaster mould, using a porcelain clay. After bisquing to 1100°C (2012°F), a colour-saturated slip was sprayed on in many layers to promote a rough textural crawling effect. The piece was electric fired to 1260°C (2300°F).

Photograph: Misun Rheem
Courtesy of Barrett Marsden Gallery, London

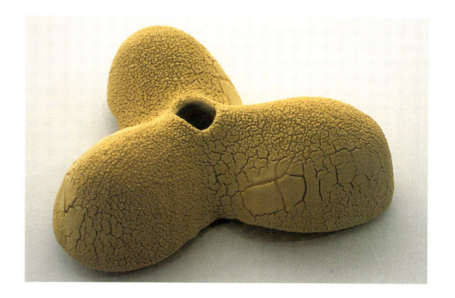

In this work my inspiration comes from nature, and an understanding of certain qualities that man, the flower and the ceramic vessel have in common: fragility, delicacy, passivity and containers of a certain spirit. My pieces can be viewed and touched from all sides — this is an ambivalence I enjoy. I admire the painter Georgia O'Keefe, the sculptor Anish Kapoor and the photographer Karl Blossfeldt.

Misun Rheem

Claude Varlan
(France)

Vessel, h. 80 cm (31 ½ in.), 1998.

Surface: Brushed and splashed coloured porcelain slips. High-fired stoneware, reduction.

This large vessel form was thrown from stoneware clay in two sections and joined. Porcelain-based slips were loosely brushed and splashed on a white slip ground, and the piece was once-fired in a wood kiln to 1300°C (2372°F).

Photograph: Georges Meguerditchian

I consider my work to be anti-ceramic in a way, a frontier between ceramics and painting. Although my shapes might be based on traditional French forms (especially those of the region of Puisaye, where I once worked), I like to break all ceramic taboos, and treat nothing as sacred – it is how you use materials that counts, and in the long run, what you choose to say with them.

Claude Varlan

Monika Debus
(Germany)

Vessel, h. 66 cm (26 in.), 2000.

Surface: Dry-brushed porcelain engobes. High-fired salt-glazed stoneware, reduction.

Slabs of stoneware clay were loosely brushed with oxide/stain-coloured porcelain engobes; first a light background wash, then a black calligraphic pattern with a thick, dripping brush. Leatherhard slabs were formed over two convex plaster shapes for the bottom half of the vessel, and broken and joined slabs formed the top. The piece was gas fired in reduction to 1140°C (2084°F), with salt introduced through holes in the top of the kiln.

Photograph: Articus & Roettgen

My work is 'visceral' rather than 'cerebral', and although I am aware of the African and Japanese vessel traditions, I do not seek to emulate them, but rather to create work that is intuitive and emotionally responsive using the simplest possible means. A shard contains the whole (I've always been fascinated by historical shards); a decoration stops, and the brushstroke continues into an imaginary void. As chance plays a large role in my painting, it seemed appropriate to choose a firing technique that reflects this approach. Salt glazing at this particular temperature achieves a subtle surface quality that enhances my painting in a delicate way, at times with extreme irregularity, which can make or break a piece.

Monika Debus

Royce McGlashen
(New Zealand)

Messages, (front piece) h. 26 cm (10 ¼ in.), w. 17 cm (6 ¾ in.), 2000.

Surface: Sprayed, sponged and brush outline slips. High-fired stoneware, oxidation.

These two shapes were constructed of rolled out slabs of a light-coloured stoneware, cut out and assembled with hand-made spouts and hand-pulled handles. A background slip colour was sprayed on the surface, with sponged slip patches applied, and fine-line brush details. The pieces were electric fired to 1190°C (2174°F).

Photograph: Royce McGlashen

Generally my teapot series develops from quick pen drawings. From there I work out a construction method. This series originated from a handbag shape, a shape of security, a shape of personal belongings, a shape of elegance. In this case I wanted to expose what was inside to the outside – notes, credit card tabs, the odd lolly paper, string, lottery tickets and messages to remind the owner, and to present them all overlapped, layered and floating – one just as important as each other, but none of them having much importance at all.

Royce McGlashen

Terry Davies
(Wales, Australia)

Sea Jug, h. 42 cm (16 ½ in.), w. 34 cm (13 ½ in.), 2000.

Surface: White engobe with overpainted black pigment. High-fired stoneware, oxidation.

This jug was slab constructed using a white stoneware body, and raw glazed with a liner glaze. The outside was then sprayed with a white engobe (80% opaque white glaze and 20% body clay), and imagery was lightly cut freehand into the surface. Background areas were pockmarked with a pencil, and the piece was lightly rubbed down when dry. Image patterns were painted with black pigment onto the slightly burnished surface, and finally the piece was once-fired in oxidation to 1230°C (2246°F).

The pivotal images in my work are sourced within a 20 square mile (32.2 square km) coastal area in west Wales. As a native I was steeped in its history, tradition and culture. Therefore from a bioregionalist perspective, not only were its flora, fauna and piscatorial elements celebrated, but also its historical and folkloric paradigms. This visual and poetic legacy is being freshly deciphered in Australia, where my inspirational sources are even more exotic. Themes from both locations provide templates for a variety of ideas I choose to express in my surface imagery.

Terry Davies

Tony Bond
(New Zealand)

Dreamkeeper III, h. 15 cm (6 in.), w. 30 cm (11 ¾ in.), 1994.

Surface: Coloured terra sigillata and sgraffito. Low-fired earthenware, oxidation.

This piece was handbuilt from a single piece of red earthenware clay, with several layers of white terra sigillata applied to the figure areas at the bone dry stage and outlined with sgraffito to the clay below. Surround areas were painted with red terra sigillata, and after electric firing to 1120°C (2048°F), indian ink was rubbed into the sgraffito lines.

Photograph: Tony Bond

Most of my ceramic work over the past decade has been body based, reflected in the form and the sgraffito imagery applied to the surface. Terra sigillata allows me to draw into, as well as paint onto the surface, which helps to integrate the narrative with the form, emphasising the communion between the two- and three-dimensional aspects of the piece. The imagery leads the eye around the form, so it's really only through investigation with both hand and eye, that the work can be fully appreciated. The form often suggests the imagery, the meaning of which may only become apparent at a later date.

Tony Bond

Edward S. Eberle *(United States)* OPPOSITE

Three Cubes, h. 48 cm (19 in.), w. 39 cm (15 ¼ in.), 2000.

Surface: Black and white painted terra sigillata. High-fired porcelain, reduction.

This porcelain shape was thrown and altered and, after final construction, handpainted using black and white terra sigillata. Various shades of thinned black, yielding grey tones, were applied as underpainting to develop field patterns and figurative motifs, using various brushes and tools (i.e. papyrus, yucca, foam, paper towels, hands, etc.). The fine-line drawing was done with fine sable brushes, with sgraffito and *mishima* inlay interventions. Detailed pattern can take up to one month to complete. The piece was once-fired in a forced-air gas downdraught kiln, in reduction, to 1250°C (2282°F).

Photograph: Edward S. Eberle

Generally, my work is about bringing together my love of form and drawing. The painting and the form are interdependent, supporting each other. The content or subject matter largely comes by way of a stream-of-consciousness process where one thing leads to another. The materials and the process allow the intermingling to take form. The work contains matters of imagination, soul, the collective unconscious, symbology, mythology, the unknown, dynamic symmetry, pattern, the human condition, birth–life–death, past–present–future, texture, and so on.

Edward S. Eberle

Roseline Delisle
(Canada; United States)

Septet 2, h. 58.5 cm, (23 in.) w. 31 cm (12 in.), 2000.

Surface: Painted vitreous engobes on raw clay. Low-fired earthenware, oxidation.

This form was assembled from wheel-thrown and trimmed earthenware sections, using specifically designed trimming tools. Vitreous engobes were brushed onto the raw clay and burnished, and the piece was slowly once-fired in an electric kiln to 1060°C (1940°F).

Photograph: Anthony Cuñha
Courtesy of Frank Lloyd Gallery,
Santa Monica, California

I became captivated with ceramics at 17 and I knew instinctively that it would become a lifelong commitment. Initially the forms were wheel-thrown vessels, progressively evolving into stacked elements of greater height and complexity. The process begins with a drawing, not unlike a blueprint elevation, which describes the component part of the piece in profile. The stripe pattern gives rhythm to the work and captures the spinning quality that refers back to its initial means of conception. In the last ten years the work has taken on an anthropomorphic personality. Consequently grouping the pieces seemed natural, in the same way that people and buildings congregate together. The work evolved from the principle of the unity of opposites: black and white, motion and stillness, strength and fragility. I draw from sources as far as ancient and primitive art all the way to the Bauhaus school of thought. Other influences are varied vessel forms such as architecture, water towers, projectiles and the human body.

Roseline Delisle

Jude Jelfs (United Kingdom)

Jug in a Striped Dress, h. 26 cm (10 ¼ in.), 1999.
Surface: Brushed and sponged vitreous engobes. Low-fired earthenware, oxidation.

This flattened jug shape was slab constructed of white earthenware. When leatherhard, coloured vitreous engobes were applied using brushes and sponge rollers. Light and heavy sgraffito lines added detail. After the bisque firing, further slip details were added, and the piece was glazed inside, and fired in oxidation to 1100°C (2012°F).

Photograph: Jude Jelfs

I am interested in the figure, in how it has been depicted in the imagery of every age and culture with such diversity and inventiveness. My pots always start with drawing, often from a model. Cutting shapes from flat sheets of clay, and painting and drawing on them with slips, is a natural progression. A two-dimensional form becomes a vessel for use, as well as for ideas. I work in earthenware for its tolerance of the demands I make on it; with slips, for their fleshy, vital quality; and porcelain, for the papery, skin-like whiteness of the fired surface. To me, the human body is a thing of wonder, a sublime piece of engineering. But I also find it rather funny. The thought that everyone is naked under their clothes never fails to make me smile. I think the great Maker in the sky has a sense of humour.

Jude Jelfs

Raewyn Atkinson (New Zealand)

A Fine Line, 28 x 14 x 11 cm (11 x 5 ½ x 4 ¼ in.), 2000.

Surface: Layered white slip with manganese-rubbed sgraffito. Low-fired earthenware, oxidation.

This bowl shape was constructed by coiling and scraping with a metal kidney tool, using a red earthenware raku clay. After several thin slip coatings to retain the texture of the clay, fine sgraffito drawing was done with a wooden skewer or needle while the slip was still soft. After bisquing, manganese was rubbed into the surface, and the piece was gas fired in oxidation to 1150°C (2102°F).

Photograph: Raewyn Atkinson

I am interested in history, New Zealand history in particular, including aspects of art – social and ecological – which I view as interrelated. Historical events happen, but how they are perceived changes. How we view the images on Mycenaean pottery and cave drawings, for example, are speculations from our present stance. Different perspectives occur not only with time, but also between cultures. It is these ideas which influence my work and these works are particularly inspired by accounts of early contact and exchange between Maori and European; events which are relevant social and environmental issues today. I like the immediacy of drawing into the soft clay or slip and how the clay records every mark. I have tried for more sketchiness in the more recent work so that the images and the forms are ambiguous, like the instability of memory and meaning.

Raewyn Atkinson

Marianne Cole (Australia)

Wattle Yellow Upright Bowl, h. 17 cm (6 ¾ in.), 1999.

Surface: Brushed bronze slip with sgraffito. High-fired porcelain, oxidation.

The bowl was wheel-thrown in porcelain clay as close to the finished shape as possible, with minimal trimming. Once bone dry, a bronze-coloured slip was applied, followed by incised sgraffito lines. After bisquing to 1000°C (1832°F), a yellow glaze was sprayed inside, and the piece was fired in oxidation to 1200°C (2192°F).

Photograph: M. Kluvanek

This work occurred through a collaboration with the painter Rita Hall for a joint exhibition. Our aim was to pay homage to and celebrate the bowl. Many hours were spent discussing and analysing each other's work, along the way becoming intimately aware of the limitations we each faced in our chosen media. Rita Hall's richly-textured collographs depicting elegant but powerful gravity-defying vessels inspired me to venture into previously unexplored areas.

Marianne Cole
From: *Ceramics Art & Perception International*, 1999, Issue 37

Louise Card (Canada)

Basket, 48 x 28 cm (19 x 11 in.) 1999.

Surface: Slip-filled sgraffito with engobes and dry glaze. Low-fired earthenware, oxidation.

This coiled pot was built free-form using thin coils working towards a large round or egg-shaped closed form. The shape was refined with a rib tool but small gaps and some of the inherent texture of the coils were left. The form was allowed to stiffen slightly and was then cut up and these part shapes were reassembled and finished with more coils or slab additions. Scratched images and texture were added at the leatherhard stage, and later filled with slip. The piece was then dried and bisque fired. A second surface consists of a thin wash of colour, usually grey, followed by brushed engobes and dry glazes. Finally, a dry matt barium glaze was brushed over the entire surface. The piece was fired in oxidation to 1180°C (2156°F).

Photograph: Westwind, Nanaimo, B.C.
Courtesy of Prime Gallery, Toronto

I consider myself a slab builder, but am enjoying working with the curved space and volume that coiling offers. The new forms reflect an interest in early historical coiled vessels. I've attempted to distil the essence of these simple functional forms by treating the surface as a skin, rather than as a glaze. A perfect pot for me would connect surface and form as succinctly as tree bark on a branch. As far as influences on my work go, I am a bit of a magpie. Some important influences are early Persian and Egyptian vessels, the work of sculptor Louise Bourgeois and painter Mark Rothko, and the utensils in the professional kitchen my husband works in.

Louise Card

Steven Heinemann (Canada)

Untitled, 26 x 18 cm (10 ¼ x 7 in.), 2000.

Surface: Layered coloured engobes, stains and sgraffito. Low-fired earthenware, oxidation.

This oval bowl form was cast from red earthenware in a mould made from a solid clay model. Slight shape alteration occurred in the soft state after removal from the mould. Stains, slips, engobes and terra sigillata were brushed on in repeated layers, with sgraffito accents. The piece was multiple-fired up to a dozen times, from 1050°C (1922°F) to 1100°C (2012°F), with many surface interventions. The repeat firing procedure is a prolonged one, which can extend over months and allow for an ongoing process of visual re-thinking and re-patterning.

Photograph: Andrew Leyerle
Courtesy of Prime Gallery, Toronto

After a lengthy period of sculptural work I 'returned' to working with bowls and open vessel forms in 1993. I'm interested in the character of contained space, and see the interiors of these vessels as a kind of terrain over which one can roam. It's also protected space in which your attention is concentrated, perhaps held for a time. So the bowls reflect my renewed interest in a more intimate framework, the power of which lies precisely in its limitations, its familiarity, its universality. In keeping with this emblem of 'craft', a heightened involvement with surface and a growing regard for the 'language' of pattern, motif, and symbol has occurred.

Steven Heinemann

Niek Hoogland (Netherlands)

Tree of Life, h. 60 cm (23 ½ in.), 2000.

Surface: Brushed and trailed coloured slips with sgraffito. Unglazed red earthenware, low-fired, oxidation.

This sculptural form was assembled from thrown, slabbed and hand-modelled components, using a coarse red earthenware with mixed grog and sand from a local tile and brick factory. When leatherhard, basic white slip areas were brushed on, and when dry, oxide-coloured slips were used to add details, using brushes and rubber bulb trailers. Graphic accents are made by sgraffito drawing through the slips using old nails. In some areas, the white slip was rubbed away to expose the red clay beneath. After bisquing, parts of the sculpture were glazed with a transparent lead-bisilicate frit glaze, and it was fired in oxidation to 1100°C (2012°F).

Photograph: Niek Hoogland

My ceramics are rooted in a long-standing slipware tradition, yet I aim to create contemporary work that is procedurally straightforward and uncomplicated. Processes encompassing a great liberty of movement allow the creation of a narrative work that is gesturally spontaneous, and often playful in aspect.

Niek Hoogland

Ann Cummings (Canada)

Artemis Fleeing the Temple, 60 x 35 cm (23 ½ x 13 ¾ in.), 1997.

Surface: Clay sgraffito with clay inlay and sprig decoration. Low-fired earthenware, oxidation.

The initial shape was made of slabbed earthenware draped over a hump mould and cut to shape. Low-relief sprig components referring to architectural or natural elements embellish the border. The central drawing motif was incised into the light clay body, and lines filled with black terra sigillata were scraped back to create a black clay inlay. Other areas were painted black and defined with a white sgraffito line. After bisquing, the rim areas were glazed, some left dry for contrast, and the piece was fired in oxidation to 1060°C (1940°F).

Photograph: Paul Schwartz
Courtesy of Prime Gallery, Toronto

Part drawing, part print, part ceramic vessel; all of these parts make up what I am trying to do in this work. Even though I have worked with clay for many years, I also perform these other artistic tasks. I feel there is a link to all of them. There is a definite reference to Greek pottery and Greek culture in the work because that is my own cultural background. In some way I also want to use the great period of Greek pottery (Attic ware) as a reference in my work, especially the use of figures drawn on the surface with terra sigillata. In many ways my work gives me a personal connection to my family and the things that meant so much to them when they left Greece. I want the viewer to make up their own story and find some sort of meaning on a universal level.

Ann Cummings

Sandy Brown (United Kingdom)

Standing Form, h. 85 cm (33 ½ in.), 2000.

Surface: Hand-pounded slabs with brushed slip and brushed and trailed coloured glazes. High-fired stoneware, oxidation.

This form was constructed from a grogged stoneware clay, loosely pounded out by hand to leave a textural surface. Slabs were casually assembled into a standing shape while still relatively soft, with further built-up sections added later for height. Thick white slip was loosely brushed on, and following the bisque firing various coloured transparent glazes were freely brushed and trailed on, as well as a zinc oxide blue glaze, and a blistering opaque tin oxide white. The piece was gas fired in oxidation to 1300°C (2372°F).

Photograph: John Andow

I seem to express dynamism, energy and freedom. I like to move my arms about, be moving around in sort of a slow dance – then I'm relaxed. Being relaxed is the key. Then I am playful, and when I am playful I feel good, and that is in the work. I like finger marks, I like accidents; I call them adventures. When I'm painting the forms I might have an idea of what the first colour will be, then after that I'm doodling, working on instinct. To feed my instinct, after the firing I look very carefully at the pieces I like most so that they are programmed into my being. Usually this is the starting point for the next ones.

Sandy Brown

Richard Parker
(New Zealand)

Cut Vases, h. 9 cm (3 ½ in.), 1999.

Surface: Brushed slip on glaze. Low-fired earthenware, oxidation.

These vases were wirecut from solid blocks of lightly grogged terracotta clay, and hollowed out. They were bisqued, glazed with a dark fritted glaze, and patterned with a loosely brushed cream-coloured slip, sinking in over the glaze. They were gas fired in oxidation to 1060°C (1940°F) over 12 hours. The matt slip surface contrasts strongly with the shiny glaze below.

Photograph: Haru Sameshima

I live in the country where my work cycle is long and uninterrupted. I try not to analyse things with the front of the brain, relying instead on a process of 'osmosis.' This allows information to soak in over many years, trusting that when its needed it will 'ooze' out, tempered by time and mixed with the life forces of my family, my teachers and all the people who have inspired me over the years.

Richard Parker

Mary Barringer (United States)

Neoribe Platter, d. 42 cm (16 ½ in.), 1998.

Surface: Textured clay, coloured slips, vitreous engobes and layered glaze. Mid-firing range stoneware, oxidation.

This piece was slab constructed, with early incised and scraped clay manipulation for texture. Layers of scraped and sanded coloured slips were applied, and after bisquing, between two and six layers of slips and vitreous engobes built up the surface further, with final thick and thin applications of layered glaze, for contrast of colour and sheen. The piece was fired in oxidation to 1222°C (2232°F).

Photograph: Wayne Fleming

For me, the surface is neither the outer skin of the form nor the final step in the process, but an integral part of my thinking and making. I introduce texture early on, to help me see the form as it evolves, and other surface elements – colour and sheen – are built up in such a way that I am still discovering the work right up to the end. What I am after is an object whose simplicity contains the monumental traces of its making, and which conveys the complex particularity of the stone as a much-used tool.

Mary Barringer

chapter four
Underglaze techniques

Underglaze techniques offer a large selection of imagery to choose from, perhaps attesting to the great popularity of underglaze techniques in general. Various clays are used in combination with brushed, painted, poured, trailed, stippled and air-brushed coloured slips and underglaze colours, under transparent and coloured glazes (usually at lower temperatures), and cobalt and oxide painting under glazes (usually at higher temperatures). Also included are *hakeme* slip and sgraffito under glaze, carved slips under glazes (transparent or salt), as well as photocopying and serigraphic screenprinting under glazes. Temperatures, atmospheres and firing methods are varied.

Stephen Bowers (Australia)

Large Platters, each d. 70 cm (27 ½ in.), 2000.

Surface: Underglaze painting on bisque under transparent glaze. Mid-firing range earthenware, oxidation.

After throwing and bisquing, these earthenware platters went through a number of stages. Once the designs were sketched on bisque, they were masked off, and the background was treated with coloured slips (airbrushed, grained, faux-marbled, sponged, etc.). The pieces were re-bisqued, after masking tape was removed. Details were then sketched and painted in, with customised brushes and oxides, stains and underglaze colours, using detailed line-drawing techniques, taking up to several weeks. A third bisquing took place, followed by a transparent glaze application and a final electric firing to 1170°C (2138°F). Gold metallic lustre was added to some areas, fired to about 760°C (1400°F), to complete the image.

Photograph: G. Hancock

I seek to create works that are both useful and provocatively decorative. I treat forms as blank canvasses upon which I explore decoration techniques that lurk on the outer limits of the potter's familiar patch. A lot of my images arise in an improvisatorial way – sort of 'stream of (un)consciousness'. A study of, and fine regard for, the mastery of various skills and techniques and their ability to communicate in form my free association and juxtapositioning. All this is finally orchestrated by an off-centre and bent sense of humour. I like fine, resolved detail and striking images on my work as this gives more satisfaction. The more you look the more you see.

Stephen Bowers

Gerald Weigel (Germany)

Steinform mit Weiss (White Stone Shape), h. 18 cm (7 in.), w. 23 cm (9 in.), 1998.

Surface: Coloured brushed porcelain slips and oxides under thin transparent glaze. High-fired stoneware, reduction.

The shape was slab constructed and modelled from grogged Westerwald stoneware, with coloured layers of porcelain slip and coloured oxides brushed into the leatherhard surface. After bisquing, the piece was spray glazed with several coats of thin transparent feldspathic glaze, and gas fired in reduction to 1350°C (2462°F).

Photograph: George Meister

My inspiration comes from nature; from stones, rocks and lava forms, and rock faces. Most of my works, although sculptural in aspect, have a double-walled construction so that in essence they can still function as containers. Artists I admire are Richard Serra and Antoni Tàpies, and among architects it is the works of Mies van der Rohe, Gropius and Foster that I find appealing.

Gerald Weigel

Woody Hughes (United States)

Tray Set, w. 56 cm (22 in.), 2000.

Surface: Polychrome slips under transparent glazes with terra sigillata. Low-fired earthenware, oxidation.

This tray set was wheel-thrown, using red earthenware that was darted and shape-altered. Polychrome slips and burnished terra sigillata were applied in the leatherhard stage, and after bisquing, fritted transparent glaze details were brushed on over slipped areas. The set was electric fired to 1060°C (1940°F).

Photograph: Woody Hughes

My work derives its inspiration from historical references and reinterpreting these influences is my passion. These influences, while based on clay, draw upon many observations, from architecture to Baroque armour. More recently the work has taken on its own order; a formal structure more unique and in response to itself than purely derivative of any particular historical period. I work in terracotta for the freedom it allows when the pieces are being created, as well as for the diversity of colour surface that lower firing temperatures permit. I am particularly interested in the formal aspects of creating, in getting each piece to work aesthetically. Balance, gesture and rhythm all function within the structure of the work.

Woody Hughes

Steven Glass (United States)

Teapot with Cups, h. 29 cm (11 ½ in.), 1999.

Surface: Polychrome slips under multicoloured glazes. High-fired stoneware, oxidation.

The works in this image are of wheel-thrown, untrimmed white stoneware, with polychrome slips loosely brush-patterned in the wet stage. After bisquing, a variety of clear, coloured, gloss and matt glazes were poured and dipped over, and the pieces were fired in oxidation to 1250°C (2282°F).

Photograph: Mike Pocklington

Through functional pieces in the realm of other time-based art forms, I seek a voice that compels and intrigues. I am inspired by the West Coast painter Richard Diebenkorn and the turn-of-the-century tonalist William Lathrop. I am also influenced by Japanese folk pottery, and harvest ideas from the tidal pools created by the ebb and flow of Anglo-Japanese style ceramics and American pioneer pottery. Working as a potter is a tended, unintended meditation in material form. I agree with the English poet Robert Browning when he writes in The Rabbi Ben Ezra: 'Time's wheel runs back or stops. Potter and clay endure.'

Steven Glass

David Miller (France)

Bath Vessel, h. 30 cm (11 ¾ in.), w. 40 cm (15 ¾ in.), 2000.

Surface: Brushed and trailed coloured slips under transparent glaze. Low-fired earthenware, oxidation.

This oval vessel was thrown and slab-constructed, using red earthenware and dipped into white slip at the leatherhard stage. Coloured stains mixed into the white slip base, slightly diluted with water, were loosely brushed over, and areas were defined with trailed coloured slip lines. After bisquing to 1000°C (1832°F), the piece was dipped into a transparent glaze, and electric fired to 1085°C (1985°F).

Photograph: by Flament, courtesy of Loes and Reinier International Ceramics, Deventer, Netherlands

In my work I try to reflect some of the cultural aesthetics of the Midi region of France, referring to landscape and deeper cultural resonances. I have attempted to synthesise some of the basic, spontaneous qualities of the local traditional slipware 'terre vernissée', and translate them into a more personal, contemporary idiom, as regards function, aesthetics, and daily ritual.

David Miller

Patrick L. Dougherty (United States)

Visage Vessels, left: h. 67 cm (26 ¼ in.), centre: h. 73 cm (28 ¾ in.), right: h. 66 cm (26 in.), 2000.
Surface: Trailed underglaze dots on black, under transparent glaze. Low-fired earthenware, oxidation.

These vessels were wheel-formed from white earthenware, and when bone dry, painted with black underglaze. Trailed coloured underglaze dot pattern was applied over the black, using a bulb ear syringe with hypodermic needles. After bisquing, a brushed coating of transparent glaze was applied, and the vessels were electric fired to 1045°C (1913°F).

Photograph: Tim Barnwell

My work serves as a means of synthesising the physical, emotional and spiritual aspects of my existence. It is an honest attempt to interpret what is in my head and heart and transform it through a physical process into a three-dimensional object. I have chosen the vessel for this purpose because I am invigorated by the making of challenging and demanding forms on the wheel, and by what I feel to be the even greater challenge of painting in the round. My imagery is an expression of who I am and how I relate to the world as an individual on conscious and subconscious levels. The painting serves as a diary in that it is a means of putting into form my visions, questions and insights at a specific point in my life's journey.

Patrick L. Dougherty

John Pollex (United Kingdom)

His Holiness the Dalai Lama, square dish, 30 x 30 cm (11 ¾ x 11 ¾ in.), 1999.

Surface: Brushed and sponged saturated colour slips under transparent glaze. Mid-firing range earthenware, oxidation.

This square dish was made from a clay slab, first rolled out on a canvas sheet, then placed in a supporting, collapsible wooden frame. Once lowered into the frame, excess clay was trimmed off, and the piece was allowed to stiffen, then brush-coated with a black slip. Saturated colour slips were sponged and brushed on and, after drying and bisquing, the piece was coated with a commercial transparent glaze and fired in oxidation to 1120°C (2048°F).

Photograph: John Pollex

I regard the visual properties of my work to be of greater interest than any functional ones. I consider myself as a painter of three-dimensional objects whereby the surface of a pot becomes the canvas. Music plays an important part in the activity of painting a pot; it helps me to create an atmosphere that reflects my mood and feelings at the time. My preference generally falls into two categories, which I like to think of as inner and outer – the inner being more contemplative (which might include Gregorian chants, Indian music and the timelessness of the Shakuhachi from Japan), the outer covers anything from modern jazz to opera.

John Pollex

Ulla Sonne (Denmark)

Argonaut-Shaped Vessel, w. 20.5 cm (8 in.), 2000.

Surface: Multicoloured slips on earthenware clay under transparent glaze. Low-fired, oxidation.

This vessel was initially thrown with red Westerwald earthenware, then cut and reassembled in sections by hand. Various stain- and oxide-coloured slips were applied in the leatherhard stage, using both brushes and a fine airbrush. Fine colour lines were added using a sgraffito needle. Superimposed layers of slip create depth and different colour tones. After bisquing (at a slightly higher temperature than glaze firing) a transparent lead-free warm-toned glaze was poured over the piece, which was then fired in oxidation to 1100°C (2012°F).

Photograph: Michael Noel

The inspiration for new designs stems from the joy and energy that arise when little miracles happen, like light colouring a landscape or the thrill of finding a fantastic shape washed up on the shore. Tiny details often catch my attention. In recent years, travels to countries with harsh nature and dramatic colours such as Iceland and Oman have provided plenty of ideas. Functionality in my objects is of great importance – most of my production is dedicated to things that can be used for serving food, and I emphasise co-operation between an item's decoration and the food that it is supposed to contain. Many items have more than one function, and they must be good to hold and feel.

Ulla Sonne

Pauline Zelinski (United Kingdom)

Platter, w. 44 cm (17 ½ in.), 1999.

Surface: Brushed underglaze colours under transparent glaze. Low-fired earthenware, oxidation.

This platter was rolled out by hand, using a white earthenware clay, and press-moulded. Once leatherhard, the rim was fettled, and up to two layers of background water-based underglaze colours were brushed on. The final overall patterns were brushed over the base colours in layers, leaving some of the background colour exposed. After bisquing, a transparent glaze was applied, and the piece was electric fired to 1075°C (1967°F).

Photograph: Pauline Zelinski

Apart from forms and patterns in nature I am inspired not only by the wonderful colours and patterns of traditional Indian textiles but also by work of the French artist Seguy – particularly the interesting use of pattern in his designs, which are rich in colour. By using underglazes, I find it is possible to achieve a type of decoration which can produce subtle and vivid hues, once enhanced by the addition of glaze. I enjoy being able to use these colours as if in a painting rather than merely as decoration.

Pauline Zelinski

Ines De Booij (Netherlands)

Block Vases, 15 x 19 x 10 cm (6 x 7 ½ x 4 in.), 2000.

Surface: Brushed coloured slips on earthenware under transparent glaze. Mid-range firing, oxidation.

These block shapes were slipcast, using red earthenware, and once leatherhard, were given individuality by the cutting out of individual openings. Once the sides of the dry vases were brushed with a coating of solid slip colour, further patterns were brushed on using more coloured slips and oxides, with occasional sgraffito detail. After bisquing, some of the interiors were coated with poured coloured glaze, and the outsides were dipped in clear glaze. The pieces were fired in oxidation to 1120°C (2048°F).

Photograph: M. Kuipers, courtesy of Loes and Reinier International Ceramics, Deventer, Netherlands

The thing I like most in my work is the painting. In order to create a lot of forms for my decoration, I choose the slipcasting technique. After designing a new model and making moulds, slipcasting enables me to make many reproductions of the item in a short time. This way I can paint and decorate rapidly: the more the better. The amazing thing is that the more I paint, the more ideas for new decorations pop up. The challenge is to give each piece a unique decoration. Thanks to the technique of slipcasting I can make this work for a reasonable price.

Ines de Booij

Irene Bell (Scotland)

Twin Ellipse, d. 45 cm (17 ¾ in.), 1999.

Surface: Underglaze pigments on greenware. Low-fired earthenware, transparent glaze, oxidation.

These plates were slipcast in white earthenware and decorated, whilst green, using underglaze. Decoration was painted, smudged, scratched and manipulated within the parameters of a black and white palette. A transparent glaze was applied and fired in oxidation to around 1100°C (2012°F) providing a seal for the still soft medium. This gives enough shine to allow the drawing maximum clarity.

Photograph: Graeme Lees

To draw onto an unfired surface presents the challenge of a tactile, yet fragile canvas. Its porous nature provides a wealth of drawing opportunity and promotes a fluency of mark making which is both spontaneous and considered. The 'plate' itself in this context disregards function, but indulges in the relationship between form and surface. My influences are eclectic. Through a long fascination with 'still life', the presence of the commonplace object has become less reminiscent of, and more evocative of, its original character. In the tradition and virtuosity of the decorated, fired surface there is an enduring pleasure in the elusive permanency of an inspired thought or response.

Irene Bell

Irene Bell (Scotland)

Alvin F. Irving (United Kingdom)

Sea Fishing Charger, d. 40.5 cm (16 in.), 1997.

Surface: Brushed underglaze colours and sgraffito under transparent glaze, gold and lustre. Low-fired earthenware, oxidation.

This large charger was wheel-thrown, using a white earthenware clay body. Once dry, all imagery was painted freehand on the main body using underglaze colours, accented with sgraffito details. After bisquing, the piece was covered with a transparent glaze and fired in oxidation to 1105°C (2021°F). Lustre and gold details were added, and the charger was refired to 750°C (1382°F).

Photograph: Andrew Morris

My work is related to environmental and social issues, relevant to my native north-west England. The imagery here depicts an allegoric satire regarding European Community fishing laws. For example, fixed to the judge's bench is a yardstick above which has been fitted an instrument to detect changes in political opinion. Indifferent fish police, dressed in fish costume, administer procedures on deck. People hauled up in nets, like fish, are judged too short, long, thin or fat, and thrown back in, and so on.

Alvin F. Irving

Anne Kraus (United States)

The Happy Spring Tulip Vase, h. 32 cm (12 ½ in.), w. 30 cm (11 ¾ in.), 1996.

Surface: Painted underglaze stains, transparent glaze on white stoneware. Mid-firing range, oxidation.

The tulip vase shape was slipcast using a mid-range whiteware body with added slipcast components. Once bisqued the piece was elaborately painted using fine brushes and hand-blended commercial colour stains and oxides. A clear glaze was sprayed over the painting, and the vase was electric fired in oxidation to 1200°C (2192°F).

Photograph: Noel Allum
Courtesy of Garth Clark Gallery, New York

'Kraus felt that these decorative objects could become potent vessels for expressing life's travails. This concept proved even more effective than the artist had suspected. By choosing the domestic forms of a cup, teapot and vase, she catches viewers off guard, not expecting these works to carry such weighty content. Furthermore, a viewer is drawn deeper into the narrative, because in order to read the vessels, one has to hold them close and therefore one's personal space is penetrated. Comprehending the work then becomes an act of intimacy and even vulnerability. By the time one discovers where the piece is headed, it is too late to back out.'

From: *Anne Kraus: A Survey* by Garth Clark

Victoria and Michael Eden
(United Kingdom)

Shallow Oval Dish, w. 34 cm (13 ⅜ in.), 1999.

Surface: Coloured transparent glazes over white slip. Low-fired earthenware, oxidation.

This oval dish was thrown using red earthenware clay and stretched on a board while still wet. Handles and feet were made by 'drawing' a handmade loop tool through wet clay, and these were then attached. The piece was covered in white slip when leatherhard, and after bisquing, yellow and blue transparent lead sesquisilicate glazes were applied to the piece inside and out. The dish was electric fired in oxidation to 1060°C (1940°F).

Photograph: Michael Eden

In the early years we experimented with a wide variety of slips and colours using traditional and non-traditional techniques to produce contemporary domestic ware. Our interest now centres on the development of slipware with reference to its traditions, our lives, and our response to the medium. We are searching for stronger, simpler forms with a greater harmony of form and surface decoration. Our study trips to Hungary, France and Portugal have formed a major part of our research. In these countries we found many links to English slipware alongside a wealth of unexpected forms and decoration. In our search for richer colours and more subtle textures we are currently experimenting with coloured glazes, lower firing temperatures and a wood-burning kiln.

Victoria and Michael Eden

Bryan Trueman (United Kingdom)

Earthenware Platter, d. 45 cm (17 ¾ in.), 2000.

Surface: Brushed, trailed and sponged coloured slips under coloured transparent glazes. Low-fired earthenware, oxidation.

After throwing and trimming, this terracotta coloured plate was covered with white slip, but not so thickly as to entirely mask the natural clay colour. Coloured slips were freely brushed, trailed and sponged in loose but controlled patterns, and after bisquing, and a transparent glaze coating, further depth of colour was added using variously applied coloured glazes. The piece was fired to 1140°C (2084°F) in oxidation, with a 30-minute soak.

Photograph: Bryan Trueman

I have lived and worked in the United States and Australia, as well as England and the influences in my works are wide and varied. From the mid 1970s to the early 1990s I concentrated on linking painting, printmaking and ceramics through a series of works which employed wax resist imagery and layering techniques. More recently I have been exploring slip-decorated earthenware, using an electric kiln. Apart from the constant source of inspiration through the visual elements in landscape, there are also traces of Oriental, medieval and Aboriginal influences that pervade my work at different times.

Bryan Trueman

Lisa Naples (United States)

Soup Tureen, h. 30 cm (11 ¾ in.), w. 38 cm (15 in.), 1998.
Surface: Painted black and white slips under transparent coloured glazes. Low-fired earthenware, oxidation.

This earthenware tureen was slab built from a red clay, using soft slabs darted at the corners with leaf shapes pushed out from inside, and added hollow slab handles. Black and white slips were brushed on at the leatherhard stage with added sgraffito details. After bisquing to 1000°C (1832°F), coloured transparent glazes were applied and the tureen was electric fired to 1100°C (2012°F).

Photograph: Jim Quale

Spending one's life as a potter is not an option that shows up in nursery rhymes with 'Doctor, Lawyer, and Indian Chief'. Without role models, it took me several years of my late teens and early twenties obsessively making pots before it actually dawned on me that maybe I could create a life with pots at the centre. Function emerged early as a priority. Utility matters to me. It doesn't need to be at the expense of beauty, but beauty must not inhibit use. There is a simple tangibility and intimacy about objects produced for the kitchen and dining room that sets them apart from other art forms.

Lisa Naples

Gail Kendall (United States)

Tureen, w. 43 cm (17 in.), 1999.

Surface: Low-relief coils and slip under transparent coloured glazes. Low-fired earthenware, oxidation.

This tureen was coil constructed of red earthenware clay, from its widest point upward, whilst upside down. Once foot and base were coiled and scraped, the piece was reversed right-side up, finished, and a coiled lid was constructed from a template. Rolled sections of clay form the handles and lid knob, as well as the cross-hatched low-relief surface pattern. The piece was entirely covered with white slip, with some sgraffito-dot details, and after drying and bisquing it was painted with clear and coloured transparent glazes. The tureen was electric fired to 1060°C (1940°F).

Photograph: Roger Bruhn

I am compelled by many streams of pottery production and tradition throughout the history of ceramics, from simple slipware and humble peasant pottery to the most elaborate and mannered industrial production of 18th- and 19th-century Europe. My works refer to manufactured ceramics in form and elaboration whilst employing techniques used in the earliest examples of pottery making many thousands of years ago.

Gail Kendall

John Calver (United Kingdom)

Pedestal Bowl, d. 42 cm (16 ½ in.), 2000.

Surface: Coloured slips under layered coloured glazes. High-fired stoneware, reduction.

This stoneware bowl was wheel-thrown, with an added thrown pedestal foot. Trailed and sponged iron and cobalt slips were applied to the leatherhard rim for leaf-and-flower-like marks, and iron and rutile slips were applied to the centre. After bisquing, the central portion was double-glazed and resisted, and various matt, coloured and transparent glazes (thinly applied) poured on the rim. Glaze and slip interaction create subtle halos of colour and bleeding. The dish was fired in reduction to 1300°C (2372°F), over 14 hours in an oil-fired downdraught kiln.

Photograph: Andrew Morris

I came to pottery as an enthusiastic hobbyist. With no formal ceramic education to guide me, and little grasp of the long tradition which informed contemporary work, I embarked on an unstructured exploration of materials and techniques. My influences have been eclectic, encompassing the slipware tradition of Staffordshire and Hungary, Scottish spongeware and Oribe stoneware from Japan. These have led me, 30 years on, to the freely-thrown, highly decorated and colourful forms which I make today. The development of my work is guided by my visceral reactions to the finished pieces, and when this intuition is reinforced by the response of my customers, I discern the direction my work should take.

John Calver

Kevin White (Australia)

Large Bowl and Large Vessel, bowl: h. 14.5 cm (5 ¾ in.); vessel: h. 24.5 cm (9 ⅝ in.), 1995.
Surface: Cobalt underglaze painting with red overglaze enamel. High-fired porcelain, reduction.

The bowl and vessel were thrown with Limoges porcelain and slightly altered when wet. Blue underglaze painting was done on the raw surface using Japanese *gosu* (cobalt pigment), ground on a glass slab, mixed with strong green tea as a medium. Varying intensities of colour depend on the ratio of pigment to water. The pieces were gas fired in reduction to 1300°C (2372°F), overpainted with red enamel, and finally refired in oxidation to 780°C (1436°F).

Photograph: Terence Bogue

My work stems from a preoccupation with functional aesthetics. Function is regarded not as an end in itself, however, but as a challenging starting point for invention within an accepted framework of constraints. Whilst the work is seldom specifically utilitarian, its character seeks to be usefully revealed. I am interested in the way useful objects can stimulate the imagination and connect the 'ordinary' with the imaginative experience; the way the magic can be made to reinvent the mundane.

Kevin White

Eric James Mellon (United Kingdom)

Theme of Mermaid, Philadelphus Ash Bowl, d. 24 cm (9 ½ in.), 1999.
Surface: Philadelphus ash glaze over cobalt, copper and iron oxide painting. High-fired stoneware, reduction.

This bowl was wheel-thrown and trimmed, using a light-coloured stoneware. After bisquing, the image was sketched onto the surface, and a wash of clean water was painted over areas to be coloured. Fine-line brush drawing and colour fill-in was done, using oxides and water: cobalt with copper for blue tones, and iron for red-brown. While the piece was still damp, oxides were lightly finger-smoothed over for better adherence and the piece was glazed over with a Philadelphus ash glaze, low in calcium, which prevents the oxides from bleeding. The piece was gas fired in reduction to about 1300°C (2372°F).

Photograph: Mike Moore

The moon goddess appears at the top of the bowl while underneath is the woman in both her mortal form and her mythological form as mermaid. The bowl embraces the idea of wife, lover, seducer, mother, tenderness, vanity, etc. The design was drawn directly from life models and is therefore not iconological. It is classical drawing relating forms on principles of composition and the use of space. The works of Raphael and Watteau are but two examples of classical drawing. This is quite different from the iconological approach to creative work which is more akin to the ideas of Cecil Collins – feelings and emotions as opposed to logic and observation.

Eric James Mellon

Phil Rogers (United Kingdom)

Squared Bottle, h. 25 cm (9 ¾ in.), 2000.

Surface: Wheel-thrown and squared with *hakeme* slip and clay sgraffito. High-fired stoneware, reduction.

This wheel-thrown stoneware bottle was squared while still on the wheel to provide distinctive faces for decoration. Thick slip was brushed on at the wet stage, using a coarse brush to impart texture in a directional stroke (*hakeme*). When the piece was closer to leatherhard, a sgraffito pattern was quickly incised through the slip, and subsequently covered with an iron ash glaze. The piece was oil fired in reduction to 1300°C (2372°F).

Photograph: Terence Bond

From the very beginning of my pottery making I was drawn to mark making in the clay as a means of decoration. My fluid wood ash glazes required ridges, incisions and hollows in which to pool and magically change colour and texture. I never learnt the complexities of pigments and brushwork. Later I turned to salt glazing and my incised, impressed, combed and faceted decoration worked here too. For me, decoration must be spontaneous, executed quickly without too much thought; an attempt to reach to the essence of something, the hand leading the brain, a single moment of expression captured in the soft clay. My time in Korea and my friend, Korean potter Lee Kang Hyo, have taught me a better understanding of the 'hakeme' approach and I use it now with deference.

Phil Rogers

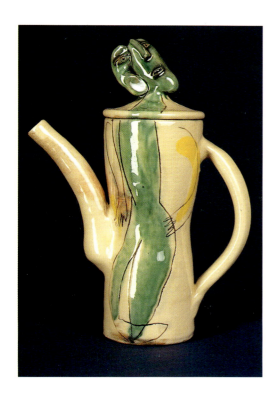

Hans Fischer (Germany)

Coffee Pot, h. 25 cm (9 ¾ in.), 1997.

Surface: White slip, sgraffito, with transparent and coloured glazes. Low-fired earthenware, oxidation.

This pot was wheel-thrown from red earthenware with a hand-modelled lid knob. After a white slip coating at the leatherhard stage, the sgraffito pattern was added and, once dry, the pot was raw glazed by pouring with transparent and coloured lead-bisilicate glazes. The pot was once-fired in a gas kiln, in oxidation, with a short period of reduction, to 1070°C (1958°F).

Photograph: Heidermann

I live in a region of Europe where there has been a long-standing tradition of earthenware influenced by many past cultures. I admire the slip and sgraffito wares that have their roots in ancient Persian and Byzantine culture, as well as those wares from central Europe (Hungary and Romania) and from Southern Europe (Italy, France and Spain). I am attempting to create work in a contemporary idiom, expressive of modern needs, but with graphic elements and techniques that are part of an ongoing, still living tradition.

Hans Fischer

Lynn Peters (United States)

Press-moulded Urn, h. 24 cm (9 ½ in.), 1998.

Surface: Black slip with sgraffito under transparent glaze. Low-fired earthenware, oxidation.

This red earthenware vessel was press-moulded, with an added coil handle. Black slip was applied at the leatherhard stage and incised with a sgraffito pattern to reveal the red clay body. After bisquing, a transparent glaze was applied and the piece was fired in oxidation to 1060°C (1940°F).

Photograph: Jeff Martin

To me the primary attraction of creating any kind of slipware is the immediacy of the process; that tactile procedural marriage between form and surface without any time lag. As a passionate dancer myself, I can make the analogy of pot making as a sort of dance of gesture and materials toward a final object, the materialisation of an ideal.

Lynn Peters

Inke Lerch-Brodersen (Germany)

Kugelform mit Quaderdekor (Sphere with Cube Pattern), h. 24 cm (9 ½ in.), d. 26 cm (10 ¼ in.), 1998.
Surface: Coloured porcelain slips with sgraffito and carving under thin transparent glaze. High-fired porcelain, oxidation.

The carefully thrown and trimmed porcelain shape was bisqued to a very low 850°C (1562°F) to remain stable enough for handling, yet porous enough to accept slip application after the bisque. The slips were made of the porcelain clay itself, with colour oxide additions of up to 20% and dried to the right consistency on plaster slabs. Slip was sprayed on, and pattern incised with a metal needle to the porcelain body below, working through successively from darker to lighter slip shades. Thin transparent glaze was sprayed overall, and the piece was fired in oxidation to 1260°C (2300°F).

Photograph: Inke Lerch-Brodersen

My intention is to marry the past with the present in creating classical shapes, and allying them with contemporary surface patterns that can confuse, or even confound the traditionality of the form, often creating a deliberate visual conflict. Hopefully, this will engender new aesthetic dialogues. The knowledge that forms in nature possess a hidden geometry became clear to me in contemplating the imagery of plant photographer Karl Blossfeldt (1865–1932) in his work Urformen Der Kunst (Archetypal Art Forms), 1929.

Inke Lerch-Brodersen

Jim Smith (Canada)

Vase, h. 37 cm (14 ½ in.), w. 18 cm (7 in.), 2000.

Surface: Slip with sgraffito drawing, sulphates and oxides under transparent glaze. Low-fired earthenware, oxidation.

This vase was thrown in sections and assembled, using a red Nova Scotia earthenware clay from a local brick factory. After dipping and pouring white slip, sgraffito line patterns were drawn through the slip into the clay, and colours filled in using sulphates, oxides and stains. After bisquing, the work was dipped in a clear glaze and fired to 1050°C (1922°F). Some of the colourants flux and move with the glaze, while others remain stiff under the glaze surface, to create a varied and voluptuous effect.

Photograph: Julian Beverage
Courtesy of Prime Gallery, Toronto

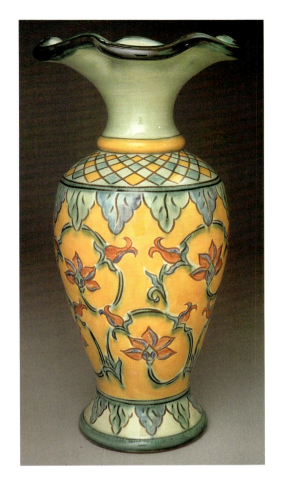

My work in slip-decorated earthenware is influenced by many of the world's great ceramic traditions. The sensuality of Persian ceramics, the luscious depth of English lead-glazed earthenware, and the joyful vivacity of Italian maiolica are tremendous sources of inspiration and delight. While acknowledging these influences through the use of historical references such as motif, colour, quality of line or glaze characteristic, I strive to create a personal and contemporary style of pottery. By combining strong forms with richly coloured and patterned surfaces, I seek to create objects that are visually and intellectually stimulating and offer the promise of domestic enrichment.

Jim Smith

Matthew Metz (United States)

Box, h. 15 cm (6 in.), 1999.

Surface: Carved terra sigillata under salt glaze. High-fired porcelain, reduction.

This covered box was wheel-thrown, using porcelain and altered off-wheel. Coloured terra sigillata, dyed with commercial stains and oxides was applied to the dry surface and carved back to the porcelain ground, just like a linoleum block. After receiving a liner glaze, the piece was salt glazed in a wood- and oil-fired kiln to 1300°C (2372°F).

Photograph: Peter Lee

My functional pots add another dimension, I hope, to the user's everyday life. Influences are diverse, ranging from early American pots, quilts, and folk art, to Asian and European ceramic traditions. The carved and drawn surfaces function decoratively but attempt to be relevant to contemporary life. Though the images resist a specific narrative reading, the iconography has been chosen for its personal resonance.

Matthew Metz

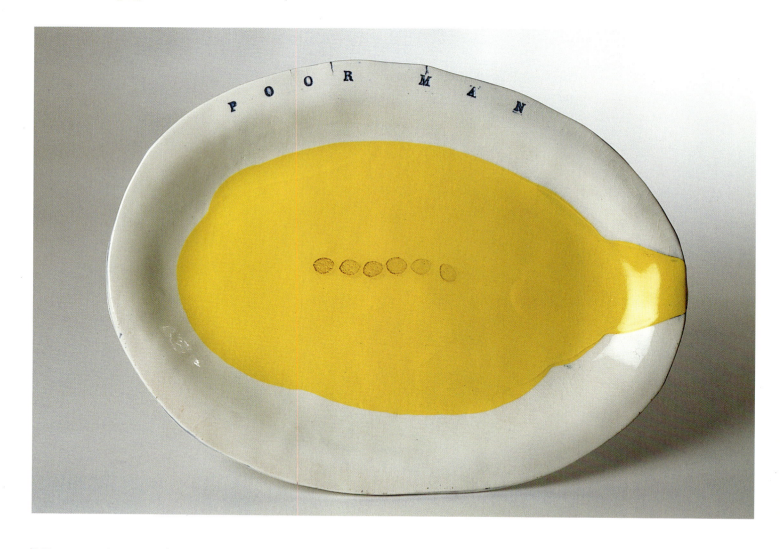

Karen Densham (United Kingdom)

Poor Man Platter, 30 x 36 cm (11 ¾ x 14 ¼ in.), 1998.

Surface: Direct photocopied image onto slip under transparent glaze. High-fired porcelain, oxidation.

This porcelain platter was drapemoulded and, once edges were smoothed, a saturated yellow slip was poured over. A row of cherry stones was photocopied, but the process was interrupted to allow the iron oxide in the ink to remain unfixed. This 'unfixed' image on paper was pressed directly onto the damp clay surface, transferring the image. Metal typeface letters were impressed around the rim, details picked out in cobalt oxide, and after bisquing and a transparent glaze coating, the plate was fired in oxidation to 1250°C (2282°F).

Photograph: Terence Bond

Poor Man is from a series which explores food; eating and cooking. Old English domestic rhymes which I remember from childhood are depicted: 'Tinker, Tailor, Soldier, Sailor, Rich Man, Poor Man, Beggar Man, Thief', associated with counting stones or pips left over after a meal, to predict who you will marry or what you will become when you grow up. The series attempts to subvert the innocent counting game by evoking ideas of class status, wealth and poverty.

Karen Densham

Ane-Katrine von Bülow (Denmark)

Three Square Bowls, h. 7 cm (2 ¾ in.), w. 17 cm (6 ¾ in.), 2000.

Surface: Serigraphic underglaze screenprint transfer under matt transparent glaze. High-fired porcelain, reduction.

These bowl shapes of slipcast porcelain were bisqued to receive an underglaze transfer pattern. A blend of oxides mixed with printing oil was silkscreened onto tissue paper, which was then turned over and applied and rubbed onto the bisque. The pieces were then re-bisqued to burn off the oil, and a thin coating of matt transparent glaze was sprayed over. Finally they were fired in gas-reduction to 1300°C (2372°F). The fired surface remains matt and stone-like over a strong contrasting black and white pattern.

Photograph: Ole Ackøy

In my serigraphic print vessels, I aim for a visual image that integrates pure vessel shape with defined geometric surface decoration. Inspiration often comes from the repeated patterns found in nature, as well as from traditional Japanese thinking and aesthetics that espouse a functionalism based on the awareness of the inherent richness of simplicity of pattern allied to function; 'design for everyday life'.

Ane-Katrine von Bülow

chapter five
Glazes used for effect

In **Glazes used for effect**, the primary visual focus (to my eye at least) is the use of varying thicknesses, colours and methods of glaze application for overall effect. Glazes are brushed, painted, poured, trailed, sponge-printed and overlapped. They can be colour saturated, or take their colour from chemical or firing interaction with one another. Included are matt surface glazes, underfired glaze, crackle glaze, crystalline and oil-spot glazes, salt glazes, raku glazes and crawling Shino glaze. Oxidation and reduction firing at all temperatures promote different surface and colour effects.

Greg Daly (Australia)

Bowl, d. 48 cm (19 in.), 1998.

Surface: Multiple-layered, resisted, brushed glazes. High-fired stoneware, reduction.

The platter, made of porcellaneous stoneware, was bisqued and spray glazed with a black feldspathic iron glaze. Areas around colours were wax-resisted, and broad brush strokes of reduced copper red and cobalt/zinc blue were applied, with multiple colour overlaps. The piece was gas fired in reduction to 1300°C (2372°F).

Photograph: R. Baader

OPPOSITE PAGE:

Glaze-on-Glaze (detail)

Sprayed green basalt/feldspar glaze, wax-resisted, with brushed over reduced copper and cobalt/zinc glaze, with added sprayed copper glaze beading over wax, high-fired, reduction.

Photograph: Greg Daly

My concern is for the whole piece – throwing, finishing, glazing and firing. Images, illusions of surface, glaze and form – all are considered equally.

Greg Daly

Paul Mathieu (Canada)

Realistic Reality, 60 x 60 cm (23 ½ x 23 ½ in.), 1988.

Surface: Painted multi-layered coloured glazes. High-fired porcelain, with metallic and colour lustre details, oxidation.

These deliberately stacked porcelain dishes were thrown and trimmed and, after bisquing, the image was carefully pencilled on. Two base glazes – one feldspathic clear and one dolomite matt – were coloured, using up to 50 tints, and the painting was applied with various brushes. Images were painted backwards, as if on glass, with forefront colours first, and background colours overall. Colours were then lightly scraped back to reveal the full image. After one oxidation firing to 1260°C (2300°F), further touching up occurred and another high-firing took place. Finally, colour enamel and lustre details completed the image at a final firing to 550°C (1022°F).

Photograph: Raymonde Bergeron
Courtesy of Prime Gallery, Toronto

This piece incorporates a large platter, a plate, a soup bowl, a salad bowl and a cup and saucer. When this particular ensemble is stacked, it displays the image of a bouquet of yellow tulips in a glass vase, within the space of a square, framed at one corner with the broken fragment of a silver frame. The image is meant to be presented and seen upside down. As the set is unstacked and each element is progressively removed, the yellow tulips in the vase will progressively die, and the petals will fall down to the ground in a logical manner, while the water level decreases in the vase. It is important in order to fully experience the piece to stack and unstack the set. In the process, the image is created and transformed, and the pottery forms, beyond function, are experienced physically through touch in space and time.

Paul Mathieu

Archie McCall (Scotland)

Celadon Pot, 20 x 25 cm (8 x 9 ¾ in.), 1999.

Surface: Poured and brushed glaze decoration with gold lustre. High-fired stoneware, reduction.

This wheel-thrown stoneware pot was bisqued and dipped into a celadon glaze. Black feldspathic glaze was poured over and colour brushwork patterning was applied using oxides and stains mixed with glazes. The pot was gas fired in reduction to 1300°C (2372°F), gold lustre details were added, and it was refired to 780°C (1436°F).

Photograph: John Gilmour

The aim of the work is to describe the natural environment of the south-west of Scotland, where I was brought up and now live. Whilst there are clear influences from the ceramics of Japan, particularly Oribe ware, the work seeks to reflect the particular nature of Scottish landscape, the lushness of our wet lands, the vigorous growth of spring and early summer and the dramatic seasonal variation. In this respect the work remains close to some of the more romantic traditions of Scottish painting or the 'decorative' painters such as Julius Bissier. The poet Tom Pow writes of the work: 'But these are not simply representations of nature in bud and flower; for the surfaces are natural, energy fields where fragile forms are threatened by rougher surfaces; great gouts of lava or wedges of cooling magma, evidence of the primal forces that have had to be harnessed and out of which this life came'.

Archie McCall

Warren MacKenzie
(United States)

Platter, d. 49 cm (19 ¼ in.), 2000.

Surface: Red Shino glaze with poured-over black glaze. High-fired stoneware, reduction.

This wheel-thrown stoneware platter with a cut foot was bisqued and glazed overall with a red Shino glaze. A black glaze was poured over, and the piece was gas fired in reduction to 1290°C (2354°F).

Photograph: John Gilmour

When I first started clay work I thought that I could integrate my painting style into what I was learning about clay work. Unfortunately my paintings were hard-edged geometric and my sense of clay was that it should be plastic and organic. Much later, through my work with Bernard Leach and long-term collaboration with my wife Alix, I turned to glazes and surface enrichment of the clay as a way to keep the brush out of my hands. Over the years I have tried to make the glaze treatment as rich as possible, while at the same time being aware of the relationship between treatment and the basic forms under it. This is where I stand today, although where I will go in the future is only a guess.

Warren MacKenzie

Yoshiro Ikeda (United States) OPPOSITE

Zen Garden, h. 53.5 cm (21 ¼ in.), w. 35.5 cm (14 in.), 1995.

Surface: Varied temperature glazes, separately fired. Mid-range to low-fired stoneware, oxidation.

This stoneware piece was coil constructed and, after bisquing, treated with glazes at various temperatures. A white, crawling high-magnesium/ gerstley borate glaze was trailed on, then fired to 1140°C (2084°F). A black and green glaze was painted on, and fired to 1080°C (1976°F), followed by a lower firing of a red magnesium/lithium glaze at 975°C (1787°F), all of the above in oxidation.

Photograph: Yoshiro Ikeda

Throughout my artistic career, I have drawn inspiration and ideas from my surroundings and experiences. My works have reflected the organic aspects of nature, the ever-changing weather, and the art of dancing. Form and surface are woven together, creating an endless line of movement. This carries the eye of the viewer, and continually provokes curiosity. In the past years, the main body of my work has been handbuilt, though I continue to wheel-throw and incorporate wheel-thrown elements in my forms. Handbuilding gives a sense of freedom and possibility. The asymmetrical aspect brings with it the eternal challenge: balance, harmony, beauty.

Yoshiro Ikeda

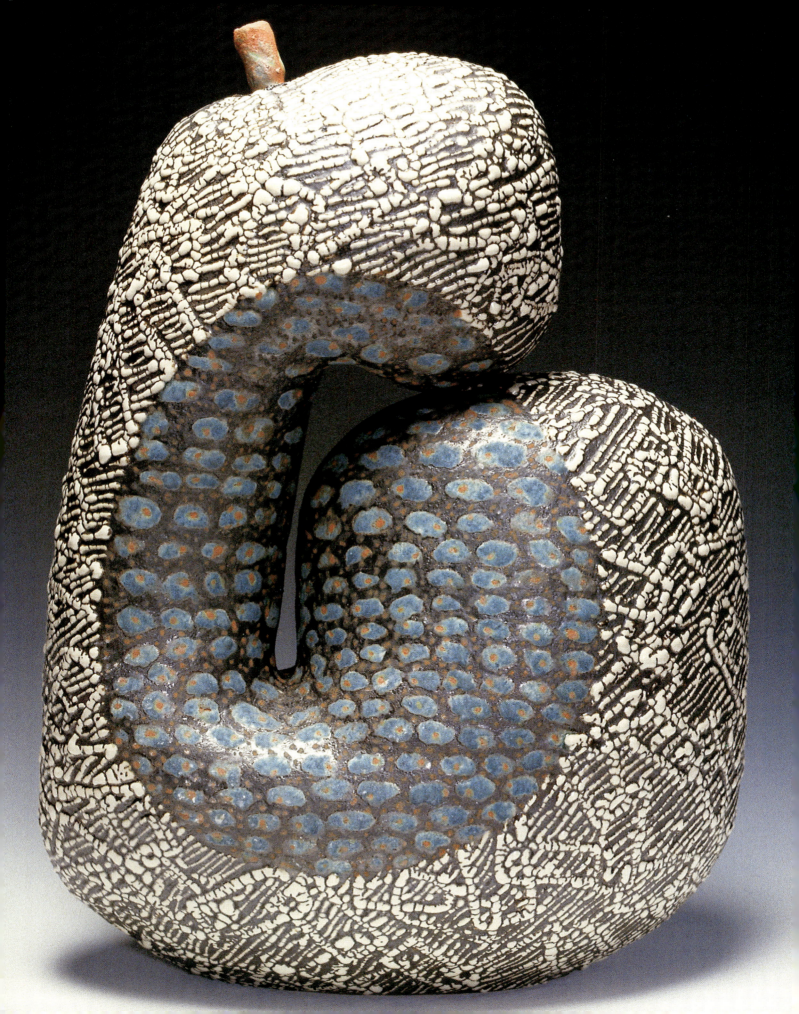

Scott Barnim (Canada)

Platter, d. 45 cm (17 ¾ in.), 1999.

Surface: Printed glaze sponge pattern and trailing, in-glaze. High-fired stoneware, reduction.

This platter was wheel-thrown using a high-firing low-iron stoneware, and after trimming, drying and bisquing, was glazed overall with a white stoneware glaze. After complete drying, a copper red glaze was applied to the border with an overlay of trailed turquoise glaze for a red flower pattern. Leaves were printed using a sponge with a chrome-green glaze on the border, and outlined with trailed cobalt glaze. The same chrome-green sponge pattern printed on the central cobalt-glazed area creates a halo around the leaves. The piece was gas fired in reduction to 1260°C (2300°F).

Photograph: Scott Barnim

I admire the works of English potters Mick Casson and Alan Caiger-Smith. My studies have led me through the practices of slipware and salt glazing to my current focus of work – a high-fired reduction 'maiolica'. The integrity of the informal pots of France and Spain continually inspire me. My imagery often reflects rural life: in the woods, on the water or in the garden. My glaze techniques allow me to handle colour with the informality of slip, and to render my themes simply. I thrive on the anticipation that results from juggling so many variables in the glazes, the application and firing atmosphere. Cooling the kiln remains an exercise in patience.

Scott Barnim

Andrew Van Der Putten (New Zealand)

Jug, h. 22 cm (8 ⅝ in.), 1998.

Surface: Copper and iron transparent glazes. Low-fired earthenware, oxidation.

The jug was wheel-thrown, using a grogged terracotta earthenware body, with slight shape alterations, and handle and spout added while still soft. The jug was dipped in white slip at the leatherhard stage, with an added stamped shell pattern. After bisquing to 1000°C (1832°F), the piece was dipped into a transparent copper-green glaze, with iron and cobalt brush drip accents, and electric fired to 1160°C (2120°F).

Photograph: Haru Sameshima

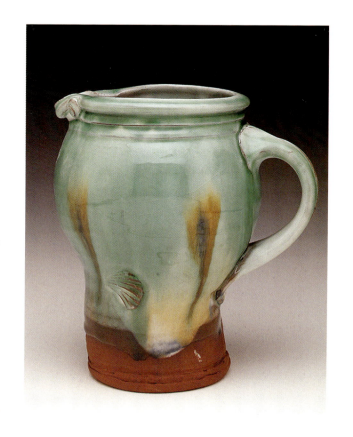

I started potting in 1967 and my enthusiasm for clay has been sustained by the fluid simplicity of the material. I am a thrower who works fast, producing quantities of work, a method by which I hopefully achieve a vitality and spontaneity. My aim is to make work in which there is a harmony of form and function, possibly with an emphasis on the form.

Andrew Van Der Putten

Gail Russel (United States)

Treasure Box, h. 8.5 cm (3 ⅜ in.), w. 14 cm (5 ½ in.), 2000.

Surface: Copper red glaze with brushed oxides, thin glaze wash, melted cones, soybeans and trailed white glaze. High-fired porcelain, reduction.

This lidded box was wheel-thrown and trimmed, using porcelain. Over a dipped copper red glaze, iron and rutile brushwork was applied, as well as a thin black glaze wash with added colour and texture provided by melted low-fired pyrometric cones, soybeans and trailed white glaze on the upper surface. The piece was gas fired in a downdraught kiln, in reduction to 1300°C (2372°F).

Photograph: Ken Van Dyne

I make pots, I make things in general, because I have to. It's just part of me. Clay and porcelain provide a means to that end. It is the incredible versatility of clay that attracts me most, with its endless possibilities of shape, colour, texture, scale and function. Thrown, classical forms speak to me most, particularly bowl forms. To me, the bowl is the pre-eminent form, it provides a base from which to explore endless shapes, sizes and uses. I employ minimal decoration, primarily glaze, colour and texture, along with some sprigging and slip trailing, preferring to let the basic form take the lead.

Gail Russel

Pippin Drysdale (Australia)

Chandni Raat, h. 50.5 cm (19 ¾ in.), 2000.

Surface: Multi-layered high-barium saturated coloured glazes. High-fired porcelain, oxidation.

This tall vessel shape was thrown and coiled and trimmed to a fine-wall thinness, using an Australian porcelain clay. After bisquing, the piece was sprayed with high-barium saturated coloured glazes, each colour individually conceived and tested for each new body of work. Due to the fineness of the porcelain walls, a drying period of 24 hours was required between colour applications. Once dry, the whole piece was covered in a paraffin/oil mixture, the wax was scored through with various tools, and after sponging down, more colour was applied to scored areas. The piece was fired in oxidation to 1220°C (2228°F).

Photograph: Robert Frith

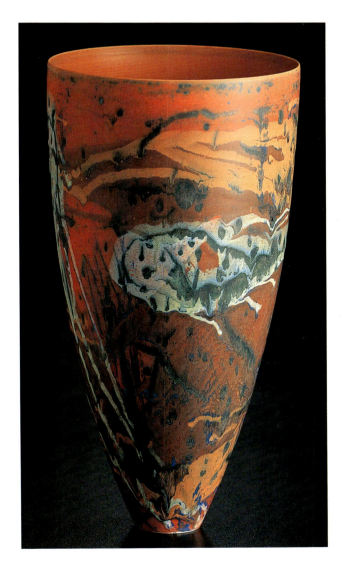

My recent travels in Pakistan and my consequent immersion in Pakistani culture have led me to completely re-examine and redefine my core philosophical and ideological views. I experienced for the first time a culture whose very existence is manifestly underpinned by concepts of unconditional acceptance, love and respect. Chandni Raat is a Pakistani formal poetic reference to the effects of moonlight on the physical structures of valley walls.

Pippin Drysdale

Steve Howell (United States)

Vessel, d. 50.5 cm (19 ⅞ in.), 2000.

Surface: Deliberately underfired, colour-saturated maiolica glaze. Low-fired earthenware, oxidation.

This vessel was constructed of slump-moulded red earthenware. After a high bisque firing to 1050°C (1922°F), colour-saturated maiolica glazes were applied by spraying and brushing, and the piece was refired in oxidation to 980°C (1796°F), well below the glaze's maturing temperature of 1080°C (1976°F), to promote a rough and textured surface.

Photograph: Randall Smith

I have always thought of myself as a painter who makes pots. My primary sources of inspiration have been the painters from the 1860s to the present. What really makes my heart soar are the colours of Monet's haystacks, the wonderful compositions of Matisse's cut-outs and the sombre intensity of Rothko's paintings in the chapel in Houston. One of the prime reasons I find such joy in painting is that the artist is responsible for every mark on the canvas. Much of ceramics depends on the process and the faith needed to produce the image, but not maiolica, especially when underglazed. These softer matt glaze surfaces draw the viewer closer to the work, and allow me to paint as on a canvas, while remaining true to the ceramics tradition.

Steve Howell

Barbara Tipton (Canada)

Red Hover, h. 20 cm (8 in.), 1995.

Surface: Dry-textured glaze with fusible sand. Low-fired stoneware, oxidation.

This teapot-shaped wall piece was first wheel-thrown from a white commercial stoneware clay, allowed to stiffen very slightly, then altered by throwing it obliquely onto a canvas-covered table. Handle and spout were pulled and altered and added to the shape. After bisquing, the body was covered with a red lead/chrome glaze, and handle and spout were covered with a magnesium carbonate/silicon carbide coating. The green spots on the body were a fusible sand mixture, applied as lumps to the raw glaze coat. The piece was electric fired in oxidation to 1040°C (1904°F).

Photograph: Barbara Tipton

For some time now I have been interested in conveying the abstract idea of containment while at the same time negating it in a physical sense. Each of the forms, which resemble cups and saucers, teapots and other vessels begin in much the same way as traditional utilitarian ware thrown on the potter's wheel. However, the original space of containment (air) has been utilised as a means of expanding, extending the exterior shell (plastic clay). It is important to me that each work begins as a fully volumetric idea; the final object serves as a graphic record of the movement of that volume. Equally important is that the form retains its visual identity as a utilitarian object. Such domestic servants are the containers and transporters of nourishment that our physical bodies require, yet they are often treated in an off-hand manner. Take one of these forms normally relegated to the kitchen, exaggerate its shape, celebrate it through colour and tactile surface, isolate it on the wall: contemporary icon.

Barbara Tipton

Harlan House (Canada)

Tulip Branch Vase, h. 41 cm (16 in.), 1995.
Surface: Crackle glaze with sgraffito drawing. High-fired porcelain, reduction.

This porcelain vase was wheel-thrown and trimmed and subjected to prolonged and careful drying before a slow bisque firing. After interior glazing and drying, the lower vase portion was dipped in a March crackle glaze, a sharp stylus was used to scratch the tulip pattern through the glaze, and glazed areas not part of the pattern were scraped way. Scratched areas were thinly sprayed over with the March glaze for a yellow hue effect. The entire base portion of the vase was wax resisted, and the upper portion of the piece was dipped in a matt crackle Xue Bai (Snow White, in Chinese) glaze. High quality india ink was rubbed into and off the background glaze surrounding the tulip pattern, for a darker crackle effect around the tulips. The piece was propane fired in reduction to 1300°C (2372°F).

Photograph: Harlan House
Courtesy of Prime Gallery, Toronto

As a painter, I know all too well that objects I see exist in a relationship to other things. As a potter, I know all too well that objects I make will exist longer than I will, and will have many relationships. It is this reality that informs me as I continue to make traditional forms that function for me. As the work moves away from me, it must be able to function in new surroundings. For this reason alone, I have chosen to involve myself with a few important words that become indelible in the work: beauty, elegance, grace, strength. If I can bring these elements together in a quiet manner I will have had a good day. If the piece provides a surprisingly good shadow, there is a bonus.

Harlan House

Peter Fröhlich (Austria)

Tropfenvase (Drop-Shaped Vase). h. 27 cm (10 ½ in.), 2000.

Surface: Zinc, silica and frit crystalline glaze. High-fired porcelain, reduction.

This teardrop-shaped vase was wheel-thrown from Limoges porcelain, and after bisquing, was sprayed with a copper-saturated zinc, silica and frit crystalline glaze. The vase was electric fired to 1300°C (2372°F), with a light surface reduction on cooling at 900°C (1652°F), and several 30 – 60 minute soaks before final cooling.

Photograph: Wolfram Orthacker

After many years of working in earthenware and stoneware, I finally decided to meet the challenge of working with crystalline glazes. Good crystals require a number of contributing factors: the correct initial glaze recipe, the right body mass and surface (especially narrow-necked pieces) and the repeated controlled holding of temperatures between 1050° and 1140°C (1922° and 2084°F), in a high-quality kiln.

Peter Fröhlich

Peter Ilsley (United Kingdom)

Porcelain Vase, h. 20 cm (8 in.), 2000.

Surface: Macrocrystalline glaze with reduced copper crystals. High-fired porcelain, reduction.

This porcelain vase, after throwing and trimming, was glazed with a zinc/copper glaze, and electric fired in oxidation to 1300°C (2372°F). The formation of crystals depends on the glaze formulation, application and the controlled firing schedule. When the temperature had reduced by about 200°C (392°F), the crystals were able to form in the glassy matrix. A further firing took place in a gas kiln up to 825°C (1517°F), then reduced down to 550°C (1022°F) over 90 minutes, to promote the red copper crystals. A small catcher dish at the base of the vase to catch the excess of the very viscous glaze was removed, after cooling, with a needle flame blowlamp.

Photograph: Peter Ilsley

I have been aware of macrocrystalline glazes for almost as long as I have been making pots – and tried many times over the years to produce them with very little success. However, some time ago I decided to make a total commitment to producing what I saw as these almost magical flower-like crystals. Although more than 11 years have gone by, every firing is still a test firing and there are always at least two test glazes in each firing. I find that as I grow, so the challenge grows. The beauty is that there is no end to it.

Koji Kamada (Japan)

Yohen Yuteki (kiln-changed oil spot) *Tenmoku Tea Bowl*, d. 14 cm (5 ½ in.), h. 6 cm (2 ⅜ in.), 1999.
Surface: Oil-spot iron-rich tenmoku glaze. High-fired stoneware, oxidation.

After throwing, trimming, drying and bisquing, this red-clay stoneware tea bowl was dipped in an iron-rich tenmoku glaze, placed in a saggar with some ash, and twice-fired in a gas kiln, first to 1250°C, (2282°F) then to 1300°C (2372°F). The oil spots occur due to large red iron oxide particles associated with impurities that decompose and move to the surface of the glaze during firing, forming lustrous self-reduced spot crystals on-surface, unable to be absorbed by the iron-laden glaze.

Photograph: Yos'ikatu Hayashi

In my early life I became fascinated by the beauty of the Yuteki-tenmoku style which has influenced my entire career. My own methods have created the effect of silver-coloured oil-spot drops on the surface. I call this 'Ginshou', meaning 'silver commendation' ('gin' means 'silver', 'shou' means 'praise'). There is a fascination in the constant variants still achievable in this long-standing traditional glaze.

Koji Kamada

Chris Weaver (New Zealand)

Teapot, h. 15 cm (6 in.), w. 14.5 cm (5 ¾ in.), 2000.

Surface: Salt-glazed ball clay slip. High-fired stoneware, reduction.

This teapot was thrown, using a white stoneware clay, and cut and altered while still on the wheel. A ball clay slip was applied, and the piece was salt fired in reduction to 1300°C (2372°F). The handle was made from strips of native Rimu wood, held in place with a length of cane.

Photograph: Chris Weaver

I rarely draw but prefer to work directly with the clay. I resolve my pieces by using what the clay reveals as I work, taking advantage of any interesting accidentals. I often add a line to accentuate a curve or distortion of the surface. It is like a continuing journey of discovery, with each new work resolved often leading to another. My interests and my influences include modern sculpture, ancient Iranian ceramics, Chinese bronzes, Japanese traditional craft and 20th-century design.

Chris Weaver

Micki Schloessingk (United Kingdom)

Tea Bowl, h. 8.5 cm (3 ⅜ in.), 2000.

Surface: Salt-glazed stoneware with poured slips. High-fired, reduction.

This tea bowl was thrown using a stoneware clay with pyrites from La Bourne in France. While on the wheel, it was faceted with a cheese slicer, and red and yellow slips were ladled on the outside while leatherhard. Dry black stain was used to accent the unslipped facets. The bowl was wood fired to 1320°C (2408°F) in a reducing/neutral atmosphere, with salt introduced after 1200°C (2192°F), and a final re-oxidation at peak temperature.

Photograph: Carrie Herbert

The salt-glazed surface creates a textured landscape that has visual depth and strong tactile qualities that invite touch. I like the surfaces to feel soft and the decoration to be both subtle and evocative. I have always been drawn to the colours of earth and fire – the myriad of reds, oranges and ochres found in a desert remind me of my original inspiration – the vivid red earth of Indian soil where I first encountered handmade pots in 1968. Wood firing and salt glazing offer the opportunity to play with the edge between control and chance. The process of salt glazing is European, first discovered in Germany in the late 14th century and in using it I feel a connection with that tradition. In terms of form and philosophy of life, my work has been influenced by an Eastern approach. I practise pot making as both a discipline and a therapy.

Micki Schloessingk

Eric Wong (Canada)

Pitcher, h. 30 cm (11 ¾ in.), d. 10 cm (4 in.), 1999.

Surface: Actively crawling Shino glaze. High-fired stoneware, reduction.

This stoneware pitcher was wheel-thrown, with an added pulled handle. After bisquing, the piece was dipped in a Shino glaze, with additional thick coatings partially ladled over. The pot was gas fired with a light reduction to 1300°C (2372°F). Where the glaze application was particularly thick, a 'controlled,' yet organic pattern of crawling occurred, revealing the clay body.

Photograph: Eric Wong

The fundamental attraction of Shino for me is its subtlety and variety of surface, so dependent on the vagaries of firing, and an inherent 'looseness' of gesture in the making procedures, a sort of controlled 'uncontrol.' There is a quality of immediate tactile intimacy that goes beyond the purely visual, an invitation to handle the rich, almost fat surface, and to bring the object into immediate and intimate use. I draw upon this very long and noble Japanese tradition to create work that is still relevant today in a personal domestic setting.

Eric Wong

Wayne Higby (United States) OPPOSITE

Monument Beach, h. 20.5 cm (8 in.), w. 21.5 cm (8 ½ in.), 1999.

Surface: Raku-fired variegated glazes. Low-fired raku clay, reduction.

This work was slab constructed, using a specially-formulated raku clay body for sufficient density and expansion/contraction capabilities. Once bisqued, various raku glazes were applied by brush in conjunction with latex resist to mask off clay areas. The piece was fired to about 1000°C (1832°F), removed hot from the kiln, and placed in a wooden box lined with damp straw, from which it was briefly removed to allow some glaze crackling and re-oxidation to occur. Glaze surface effects depend on the careful process of removal from kiln, judging of external temperatures, length and quality of reduction and re-oxidation, etc.

Photograph: Brian Oglesbee

Open and expansive, the landscape of America has, for generations, reflected the promise of a New World. Celebrated by artists, the panorama of American nature has been transformed into a symbol of diversity and a spirit of opportunity. From sublime vistas to the intimacy of gentle pastures, the American landscape inspires longing and hope. My ceramic work has become an extension of the tradition of American Landscape Art. By process it is an analogue to nature herself – earth, water and fire team together to bring forth mysteries of place.

Wayne Higby

111

chapter six

In-glaze painting

In-glaze painting techniques are especially close to my heart, and yet this comprises one of the smaller chapters. In-glaze painting refers to the technique of painting stains or oxides directly onto the raw glaze (whether applied to bisqueware or greenware). Surface pattern fuses into the glaze (in-glaze) upon final firing. Some underglaze painting under transparent glaze can often resemble in-glaze painting, and sometimes careful examination is required to differentiate. Low-fired in-glaze painting (usually maiolica,[1] or tin glaze) here includes wet-blending and sgraffito, brush line-drawing, on-surface dry smudging, cobalt in-glaze painting, use of *coperta* (or *crystallina*), use of black underglaze and, in the high-firing range, the use of oxides, both in oxidation and reduction.

[1] I use the term 'maiolica' (not 'Majolica') to refer to the techniques and products of low-fired, tin- or zircon-opacified glazed earthenware. 'Majolica' (although often used interchangeably with 'maiolica') in my opinion more correctly refers to the ornate Victorian wares produced by the Minton factories in England during the mid-1800s.

Matthias Ostermann (Canada)

Adam and Eve (plate detail), d. 28 cm (11 in.), 1995.

Surface: Multi-layered wet-blended stains and sgraffito on maiolica glaze. Low-fired earthenware, oxidation.

This plate was made of slab-rolled white earthenware draped over a bisqued clay mould. After bisquing and glazing with a zircon-opacified glaze, coloured stains and oxides (copper carbonate in the tree) mixed with frit and water were painted freehand on-surface, and quickly wet-blended with stiff brushes. A fine-line sgraffito drawing through the colour and the glaze (but not through to the body) defines the image. The plate was electric fired to 1040°C (1904°F).

Photograph: Jan Thijs
Courtesy of Prime Gallery, Toronto

I have always had a love of stories and legends, a legacy from my mother who was a professional 'raconteuse' in Germany. There is something endearing about Adam and Eve, the so-called originators of all our woes. Reaching for the apple, wearing their modest fig leaves, they portray the same kind of innocence and naïveté as their counterparts on 17th-century English Delftware chargers.

Matthias Ostermann

Terry Siebert (United States)

Renaissance Orchard Pitcher, h. 45 cm (17 ¾ in.), 1992.

Surface: Fritted colour stains brushed on maiolica glaze. Low-fired earthenware, oxidation.

The thrown and trimmed pitcher was bisqued and carefully dipped in tin glaze, with all decoration painted on-surface with stains and oxides, mixed with water and glycerine to promote even flow and prevent smudging. Both bisque and glaze firing were to 1060°C (1940°F), for optimal clay clearance and glaze fit.

Photograph: Roger Schreiber

I am a potter who likes to paint and has a passion for colour. I continue to be inspired by the intricacies of nature and the rich traditions of maiolica pottery. I love the meditative process of immersing myself in nature and sketching my observations. I admire the exotic form and ornamentation of Persian ceramics with its highly abstracted, imaginative, plant-derived designs. I also enjoy Spanish lustreware with its lively, calligraphic brushwork and designs utilising the interplay of positive and negative space. Ultimately, the process of pottery making is a means of connecting myself to the natural world, other cultures and artists before me, and to those who now find meaning in my work.

Terry Siebert

Daphne Carnegy (United Kingdom)

Jugs, (tallest) h. 30 cm (11 ¾ in.), 1995.

Surface: Tin glaze with stain- and oxide-painting. Low-fired earthenware, oxidation.

These jugs were wheel-thrown using a red earthenware body, and after bisquing to 975°C (1787°F), were dipped in a lead/borax-based tin glaze. Patterns were lightly sketched in with a pencil, and filled in using oxides and commercial stains mixed with water. The pieces were fired in oxidation to 1080°C (1976°F).

Photograph: Stephen Brayne

I was first attracted to earthenware when I went to live in France and was exposed to country pottery, mostly slipware, but also faïence (tin-glazed earthenware). I liked the eminently functional forms, the unpretentiousness of the decoration. But in particular I was drawn to the colour possibilities and the 'separate' surface quality of the glaze, inviting articulation and exploration in the decoration. Other influences are early Italian painting for colour palette, Spanish/Dutch still life for detail and realism, Cézanne for his fruit paintings, African textiles and Mimbres pottery for setting the standard on design. In tin-glaze tradition, I am most drawn to early Italian, Hispano-Moresque and Islamic pieces.

Daphne Carnegy

Marino Moretti (Italy), Victor Greenaway (Australia)

Fish Bowl (detail), h. 25 cm (9 ⅞ in.), 1999.

Surface: In-glaze line drawing and painting on porcelain. High-fired, oxidation.

This work was created in Australia in the studio of Victor Greenaway, who collaborated as thrower with Moretti as painter. The bowl was made of porcelain and, after bisquing, it was covered in a white opaque glaze. The imagery was painted on with various oxides and small brushes, using a line-drawing technique, with diluted brushed colour areas. The piece was fired in oxidation to 1265°C (2309°F).

Photograph: Marino Moretti

I was initially much influenced by the iconography of traditional local historical maiolica, especially from the extensive collections of my father and grandfather. I feel that I have absorbed a particular tradition, notably that of medieval maiolica decoration from Orvieto (my own area) as well as from Viterbo and Alto Lazio. My current challenge is to translate this rich visual heritage into a contemporary idiom that is entirely my own.

Marino Moretti

Walter Ostrom (Canada)

Hortus Testudinei (detail), 35 x 42 x 72 cm (13 ¾ x 16 ½ x 28 ¼ in.), 1999.

Surface: Tin glaze (maiolica) with in-glaze decoration. Low-fired earthenware, oxidation.

This piece was press-moulded from local earthenware clay and covered with a white engobe. After bisquing, the maiolica border was poured and decorated, using fine brushes, stains and oxides. This border was then waxed over and the runny glaze was sprayed on. The piece was electric fired to 1040°C (1904°F).

Photograph: Ying Yueh Chuang

The genus Testudinei and the genus Rhododendron continue to co-exist after 250 million years. The choice of earthenware clay is self-evident, but the play of glaze types and their physical characteristics (i.e. 'fake' ash with 'fake' porcelain, 'real' fluidity with 'real' viscosity) makes it ambiguous. However, the schematic images of the elepidote rhododendrons ornamenting the carapace of the realistically-rendered tortoise make clear this piece is about time and duration rendering the question of 'fakeness', in terms of glaze likeness and history, mute.

Walter Ostrom

Matthias Ostermann (Canada) OPPOSITE

Atlas Candle Holder, h. 26 cm (10 ¼ in.), 1997.

Surface: Coloured stains on maiolica glaze with dry-blended contour smudging. Low-fired earthenware, oxidation.

This candle holder was constructed of two wheel-thrown sections (top and bottom) joined by a hollow slab shape, to create a two-sided image. After bisquing and tin glazing, the figure was outlined with a calligraphy brush and a black stain/frit/water mixture and contours were dry-smudged on-surface with a finger, for an effect of volume. Background colours were painted in, and the piece was electric fired to 1040°C (1904°F).

Photograph: Jan Thijs
Courtesy of Prime Gallery, Toronto

I have always had a fascination for Greek myths, and the tempestuous pantheon of Greek gods and goddesses. Their overblown human characteristics, such as envy, spite, generosity and implacable hatred (rather than abstract positive virtues), were directed both towards unfortunate humans and their own kind. In this case, poor Atlas, one of the old Titans, was condemned to bear forever the weight of the heavens on his shoulders. I have reprieved him by giving him the weight of a candle only.

Matthias Ostermann

Daniel Kruger (Germany)

Two Covered Dishes made at the European Ceramics Work Centre, Netherlands, each h. 22 cm (8 ⅝ in.), w. 20 cm (7 ⅞ in.), 1995.

Surface: Tin-glazed earthenware with cobalt in-glaze painting. Low-fired, oxidation.

These two lidded jars were handbuilt of earthenware clay, bisqued at 1100°C (2012°F). Cobalt in-glaze painting was applied to the off-white tin glaze, which was then covered with a thin transparent *coperta* coating. Glaze firing was in oxidation to 1060°C (1940°F).

Photograph: Peer van der Kruis

My choice of technique has to do with an interest and fascination with historical examples with which I have become familiar and which I admire. These examples (in this case Dutch Delftware) although essentially European, show a derivation from the much-admired and emulated Chinese porcelains. A further interest of mine is the juxtaposition of images or symbols: a contemporary image with a historic pattern; realism with illusion; the customary with the unexpected.

Daniel Kruger

Alexandra Copeland (Australia)

Marie Antoinette with her Hairdresser, Vanity Series, Platter (detail), d. 65 cm (25 ½ in.), 1996.

Surface: Tin-glazed earthenware with cobalt in-glaze painting. Low-fired oxidation.

This wheel-thrown earthenware platter was bisqued and glazed with tin glaze (maiolica), and all painting was completed freehand with cobalt stain onto the glaze surface. Yellow pigment was carefully applied as a background, and the platter was gas fired in oxidation to 1000°C (1832°F).

Photograph: Andrew Clarke

In 1999 Australians voted against becoming a republic and kept Queen Elizabeth as Head of State. Our queen was lucky – Marie Antoinette lost her head. In the long and often emotional debate leading to the referendum, I produced a series of large platters (Vanity Series) depicting aspects of the bloody and wonderful French Revolution. The cobalt blue image was drawn directly onto the raw tin glaze with no prepared outline. I enjoy working in 'premier coup' (pun intended) – it is both risky and thrilling. I chose an orange/yellow background for a piquant contrast with the traditional blue and white delft-like palette, emphasising the contemporary slant of a historical theme.

Alexandra Copeland

Connie Kiener (United States)

Yin Yang Weather, d. 56 cm (22 in.), 2000.

Surface: Painted coloured stains on maiolica glaze with transparent glaze coating. Low-fired earthenware, oxidation.

This large platter was made in a slump-mould of earthenware clay, and bisque fired high to 1135°C (2075°F). A zircon-opacified maiolica glaze was sprayed over, and the platter was decorated in-glaze in detail with suitably fluxed colour stains. A thin, clear *crystallina* glaze, fluxed to mature at a slightly lower temperature than the maiolica glaze below, was sprayed overall, and the platter was fired in oxidation to 995°C (1823°F).

Photograph: Bill Bachuber

I am visually voracious and am constantly looking around – the natural world is the largest pool that I draw from. However, I am captivated by other forms of human expression, such as old maps, basketry, heraldic symbols, repeat patterns, ancient jewellery, fans, etc. Currently I am intrigued by William Morris design, and the use of primary and secondary layering of motifs. I use imagery as a metaphor to tell my stories. For instance, in my most recent platter series, I've used the bird riding on or carrying large feathers to comment on contemporary transportation modes. The feather is the antithesis of the fossil fuel vehicle.

Connie Kiener

Deborah Kate Groover (United States)

Vase, h. 40.5 cm (16 in.), w. 25.5 cm (10 in.), 1992.
Surface: Layered white over black tin glaze with resist and in-glaze painting. Low-fired earthenware, oxidation.

This vase form was constructed of earthenware slabs, maintaining a loose, organic shape. After bisquing, a black glaze without opacifier was applied, some black areas were resisted, and a white maiolica glaze was applied overall. Coloured fritted stains were brushed on, and the piece was glaze fired in oxidation to 1060°C (1940°F). The more viscous black glaze beneath the white promotes a light blurring of the image, as well as letting dark spots break through the colour areas.

Photograph: Walker Montgomery

My work tends to be largely narrative – I have studied classical mythology, comparative religions and southern literature. I concluded long ago that in telling a story, knowing precisely where the reality ends and the myth begins is not necessarily the most important part of the story. My narratives combine personal iconography and classic archetypes.

Deborah Kate Groover

Laurence McGowan (United Kingdom)

Rimmed Dish, d. 29 cm (11 ¼ in.), 2000.
Surface: High-fired zircon-opacified glaze with in-glaze painting. Stoneware, oxidation.

This dish was made of wheel-thrown light stoneware, and glazed after bisquing with a Cornish stone/dolomite zircon-opacified glaze. In this case the traditional low-fire maiolica technique has been translated to a higher temperature range. Brushwork decoration was painted freehand, using a mixture of oxides and stains, with added gum arabic to assist the flow. The piece was electric fired to 1260°C (2300°F).

Photograph: Magnus Dennis

I regard decorating pottery as an adventure and an exploration of both the universal self and the pot's form. It is also a craft with its own disciplines, clear objectives and considerations. True decoration is not some ill-considered afterthought. Indeed, the only valid reason for putting brush to pot is to echo, amplify, enhance and complement the essence of the form. Decoration is therefore, functional. Just as wheel-thrown forms are abstract symmetrical patterns, so is my decoration. Just as many forms are reminders of the natural world, so is my decoration. I bear in mind that the word 'decoration' comes from the same root as decorum with all its implications of fitness for purpose, politeness, good manners and quiet poise.

Laurence McGowan

Sam Uhlick (Canada)

Cup, d. 12 cm (4 ¾ in.), h. 11 cm (4 ¼ in.) 1995.
Surface: Hand-milled cobalt pigment with sgraffito on feldspathic glaze. High-fired stoneware, reduction.

The cup was wheel-thrown from quarried grey stoneware clay, slip-mixed and stiffened in sun pans. Once bisqued, the cup was dipped in a feldspathic glaze, also quarried and ball-milled. The cobalt pigment – applied with a hand-trimmed brush, with light sgraffito details – was made from oxidised and ball-milled cobalt metal mixed half/half with a native ball clay. The green chrome pigment accents were applied with a squeeze bottle, and the piece was lightly reduced in a gas firing to 1300°C (2372°F).

Photograph: Jan Thijs

I love the physical work of making pottery, throwing most of all, but also preparing clay, building and repairing equipment. The cycle of work has an intangible influence on my pottery. Much of this stems from the legacy of Michael Cardew with whom I worked for some time. The feel of a pot; weight, form and balance, are very important to me. The kind of pottery that gets my adrenaline pumping is antique Oriental pottery, and this was the reason for my first visit to Japan when I was 19. My work is still influenced by this pottery, although less by tea ceremony tradition now than by tea party tradition. There is a dignity and depth in folk pottery that is, for me, very attractive. I don't attempt to create perfection in my own work or contrive imperfection, but there is a simple beauty in ordinary pots that I hope to emulate in my work.

Sam Uhlick

Seth Cardew
(United Kingdom)

Painted Bird Plate, d. 30 cm (11 ¾ in.), 1993.

Surface: Painted iron/cobalt pigment on Shino glaze. High-fired stoneware, reduction.

This thrown stoneware plate was made of a blend of local fire clay, ball clay and kaolin. Once raw-glazed by dipping into a Shino glaze, it was brush-decorated using an iron/cobalt pigment mixture. The piece was wood fired in a downdraft kiln to 1300°C (2372°F), with reduction occurring just over 1000°C (1832°F).

Photograph: Jan Thijs

Inspiration for my pots comes from the materials of which they are made. The materials are obtained from the nearby countryside and milled at the pottery. The decorations are inspired by music; that of birds singing, and the texts of the composers of antiquity, who wrote for the pure female voice. The effects of the glazes are enhanced by firing the kiln with wood, for showers of sparks settle on the pots each time the kiln is stoked and in this manner the pots are subjected to the comments of the flames; sometimes favourable, and sometimes not. One of my favourite contemporary potters is Sam Uhlick whose work always feels just right in the hand – he brought me to appreciate the art of touch in pottery. His work enhances and transcends the simple dogmas of usefulness in pottery, to a level of pleasure in use.

Seth Cardew

Beate Andersen (Denmark) OPPOSITE

Folded Form, h. 16 cm (6 ¼ in.), 1998.

Surface: Multi-layered matt-glazed stoneware surface with brushed oxide decoration. High-fired, reduction.

This organic stoneware shape was wheel-thrown and altered, with an added slab base construction. After bisquing, several layers of matt glaze were sprayed on to create a depth of surface, and pattern was brushed on using basic oxides, and following the rhythmic surface of the piece. It was gas fired in reduction to 1300°C (2372°F).

Photograph: Ole Haupt

One of my inspirations for the use of flowing shape and rhythmic pattern was the beautiful walls of a Tibetan monastery that I visited in 1998. Study trips to India and Nepal have also provided much food for aesthetic thought. As I see it, man has at all times and in every geographic location on earth enriched buildings, functional objects and tools with pattern and ornament, made up of the same simple lines, dots and basic geometric figures. Individuality occurs through the added imprint of the particular culture. These archetypal patterns must be a natural expression of our common humanity.

Beate Andersen

chapter seven

Resists and masking techniques

Resists and masking techniques are those making use of some kind of masking or resisting process to separate distinct fields of colour and pattern. Some of the resists include: shellac resist on dry clay for surface erosion and separating soluble metal salts, wax, water-based wax emulsion, *cuerda seca* technique, latex, paper stencils and tape resists. Some resists are used under glaze, some separate layers of glaze, others resist glaze in combination with flashing slips and soda firing. Again, all types of clay, firing methods and temperatures are included, in both oxidation and reduction.

Peter Fraser Beard (United Kingdom)

Block Vessel, h. 52 cm (20 ½ in.), 1999.

Surface: Wax-resisted layered glazes. High-fired stoneware, oxidation.

This vessel was slab constructed of Molochite-grogged stoneware and refined in the leatherhard stage. After bisquing to 1000°C (1832°F) it was dipped in a matt barium glaze and patterned with water-based wax resist. This was allowed to dry before applying several layers of low-temperature oxide-stained alkaline glazes of various colours. The piece was fired to 1300°C (2372°F) in oxidation. The final surface texture was due to layered glaze thickness.

Photograph: Peter Fraser Beard

The main objective of my work is to produce beautiful objects that are very contemporary, but nonetheless have an allegiance to history, giving them a timeless quality. Landscape in all forms is my main source of inspiration, along with the art of ancient Egypt.

Peter Fraser Beard

Arne Åse (Norway)

Bowl, h. 30 cm (11 ¾ in.), w. 30 cm (11 ¾ in.), 1994.

Surface: Shellac-resisted low relief with etched and painted metal soluble salts. High-fired porcelain, reduction.

After throwing, trimming and drying, those areas of porcelain to remain in high relief were covered in shellac, and low-relief areas were wet-sponged away. White areas were re-shellacked, and in a batik-like process, successive layers of colour over shellac-resisted areas were built up. Colours consist of soluble metal salts, in this case an overall wash of gold chloride, partly resisted, then covered with a potassium dichromate solution which presses the gold into the clay. More resisting took place and a light brown iron chloride solution was painted on. Colour variations occur where colours overlap, and texture and translucency are promoted by the varying thicknesses of surface. The piece was fired once, upside down on a clay cone to maintain its shape, in an electric kiln reduced with gas, with a final firing temperature of 1230°C (2246°F).

Photograph: Glenn Hagebu

There is a Norwegian folk art called 'rose painting' which is pervasive in traditional costumes, wood carving and painting, silverwork and decorative painted domestic architecture. Like Op artist Vasarely, I have taken apart traditional motifs and reassembled them into a new 'optic geometry'. It is a new visual language, a high-tech way of looking at traditional folk art, much in the way that contemporary jazz music breaks down and reassembles classical music structures.

Arne Åse

Astrid Gerhartz (Germany)

Cylinder, h. 19 cm (7 ½ in.), w. 17.5 cm (7 in.), 1997.
Surface: Shellac-resisted clay relief and brushed coloured soluble salt oxides. High-fired porcelain, reduction.

The shape was thrown and trimmed in porcelain and once dry, shellac patterns were applied, which resisted wet-sponging. This process was repeated two to three times, each shellacked area creating a raised relief pattern. Thin, almost translucent areas occur where clay has been washed away the most. After bisquing, the lower half of the piece was brush-painted with soluble salt oxides, including cobalt, chrome, copper, iron, nickel, gold and vanadium. A reduction gas firing took place at 1260°C (2300°F).

Photograph: Foto Gross

About porcelain, what can I say? Whiteness, transparency, hardness, shape, colour, gesture, construction, complexity, restraint, care, concentration, decisiveness, lightness, clarity, poetry.

Astrid Gerhartz

Ulrike Friedemann (Germany)

Teapot, h. 19 cm (7 ½ in.), 1998.

Surface: Shellac-resisted low-relief porcelain. High-fired, oxidation.

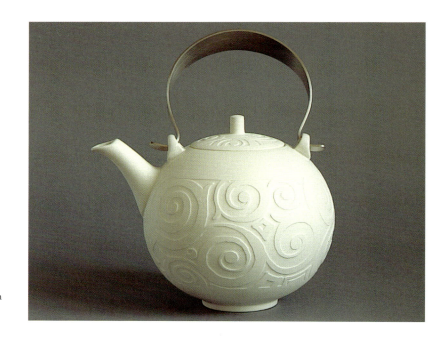

The porcelain shape was slipcast in self-made plaster moulds. Once components were assembled, all surfaces (including spout and knob) were shellacked in the dry state, as well as the patterns that remain raised. Unshellacked areas were sponged down to create an eroded low-relief. The shellac burned off during bisquing, and the interior was glazed, prior to an oxidation firing at 1300°C (2372°F). Finally the outside surface was polished by hand to a soapstone-like finish, and a stainless steel handle was added.

Photograph: Ulrike Friedemann

In our studio in Halle we produce one-off pieces and functional repetition ware. We work through all the inherent processes, from design through mould-making, to final decoration and finishing, and our primary mandate is to produce work that is not only aesthetically pleasing but also eminently functional and serviceable.

Ulrike Friedemann

Jeff Oestreich (United States)

Tea Bowls, each h. 11 cm (4 ¼ in.), w. 9.5 cm (3 ¾ in.), 1997.

Surface: Wax-resisted panels of copper and iron-breaking glazes. High-fired soda-vapoured stoneware, reduction.

These stoneware tea bowls were thrown, trimmed, and faceted. They were decorated with green chrome-bearing glaze, applied with finger and brush, resisted with wax and dipped into an iron-bearing glaze (left) and into a copper- and iron-bearing glaze (centre and right). They were fired to 1260°C (2300°F) in a soda kiln, with limited amounts of soda to promote varied surfaces.

Photograph: Jan Thijs

I have chosen the soda-firing surface for its variety and its more random distribution than that of a salt surface. The pot records the position in the kiln, thus the stacking is critical. Surface effects, enhanced by wax resist to contrast base clay with glaze, can range from a heavy orange peel surface to light flashing, all on the same piece.

Jeff Oestreich

Royce McGlashen (New Zealand)

Tea Party, h. 50 cm (19 ½ in.), w. 40 cm (15 ¾ in.), 1996.
Surface: Wax-resisted outline drawing with overlaid slips. High-fired stoneware, oxidation.

The teapot shape was made from slabbed stoneware well grogged for contrast between clay body and the parchment-like slip panels. After bisquing to 950°C (1742°F), hot wax was used to outline the decoration on the panel paintings, and coloured slips were applied by dabbing with a sponge, followed by some brush strokes for further definition. The piece was electric fired to 1260°C (2300°F).

Photograph: Royce McGlashen

This series was a continuation of my exploration of the teapot theme as a production potter. I throw and assemble many teapots, and I wanted to take the body and appendages of the teapot (handle, spout, lid), forget the practical use, and create an art form from all these elements. The teapot is the picture frame with loosely-decorated panels positioned on each side of the form. The decoration celebrates the custom of tea drinking.

Royce McGlashen

Jeff Irwin (United States)

Aspen Day and Night Teapot, h. 46 cm (18 in.), w. 40.5 cm (15 ¾ in.), 1997.
Surface: Wax drawing on glaze with black glaze and sgraffito. Low-fired earthenware, oxidation.

This teapot was handbuilt, using a white earthenware clay, slab, coil and pinch construction. After bisquing, it was painted with a white satin glaze, and all white areas were painted with wax, after an initial pencil sketch on-glaze. A black satin glaze was painted around waxed areas, with occasional white sgraffito detail, and the wax was scratched through for added black line detail. The piece was electric fired to 1060°C (2300°F).

Photograph: Jeff Irwin

I create my work to examine and communicate environmental issues that are important to me. Utilising the tree image as a metaphor for nature, I examine the uses and abuses we impose upon the natural world to make our lives better. I often integrate the human presence with the narrative through symbolic imagery. Though a recognisable figure is rarely depicted, I utilise images that refer to this presence. The contradiction of our love for the natural world and our simultaneous need to exploit it plays a constant role in developing the work. These conflicts and contradictions encourage an inquisitive atmosphere and direct the viewer to examine the ambiguities of reality, illusion, and perception.

Jeff Irwin

Chris Thompson (Canada)

Compass, d. 69 cm (26 ¾ in.), 1998.
Surface: Wax-resisted airbrushed stains, raku-fired. Low-fired earthenware, reduction.

This piece was slab constructed of raku clay stretched and rolled into a large sheet, with a visible canvas-imprinted surface. After bisquing, the platter shape was coloured by airbrushing stains and underglaze colours, having first applied wax resist to those areas that would naturally smoke-fire from grey to black from the reduction effects of raku. Brown tones were created using terra sigillata, and varying thicknesses of transparent glaze were applied, to promote both matt and shiny surfaces. After raku firing to between 850° (1562°F) and 950°C (1742°F), the piece was removed from the kiln and placed in a sawdust/sand mixture to create various smoked effects.

Photograph: Chris Thompson
Courtesy of Prime Gallery, Toronto

My initial interest in raku was for the interaction of rich colours in conjunction with the smoky, more illusive surfaces promoted by raku firing. Line and pattern create contrasts to the forms, and living on Toronto Island surrounded by water has definitely influenced my sense of colour and light. My surfaces of inspiration are diverse – travel, landscape, influences from art and architecture – and they all filter through into some kind of coherence of image related to form.

Chris Thompson

Will Levi Marshall (Scotland)

Large Dish, d. 60 cm (23 ½ in.), 1998.

Surface: Glazes resisted with tape and wax emulsion with added silkscreen transfers. High-fired stoneware, oxidation.

This large wheel-thrown platter was fired to a soft absorbent bisque, to better absorb several thin layers of glaze. After pencil sketching onto the bisque, areas were masked with tape, glaze was ladled over, and covered with a dilute wax emulsion. Tape was removed, and the next glaze applied. The plate was fired to 1275°C (2327°F) with a long soak in oxidation with slow cooling to promote matt glazes. An overglaze silkscreen print transfer in black was fired to 750°C (1382°F).

Photograph: Will Levi Marshall

I love all kinds of pots: wood-fired, salt-glaze, slipware, raku, reduction – the list is endless. I am at present enjoying the unusual colours and textures achievable with oxide flux combinations at stoneware temperatures. The wheel proves to be a challenging vehicle to prepare a canvas, yet within the framework of function. More broadly, my concerns are centred around how line affects form, creating a relationship between the static and the dynamic.

Will Levi Marshall

Mark Pharis (United States)

Pitcher, h. 33 cm (13 in.), w. 38 cm (15 in.), 2000.
Surface: Masked and resisted slips and glazes. Low-fired earthenware, oxidation.

This pitcher was slab built, using a sketched paper pattern as a template. After bisquing, the spout was masked, dipped in calcined white slip and white glaze, and waxed over. The vessel itself was also dipped in white slip, wax dots painted on, and dipped again into a yellow lead/potassium-dichromate glaze. The pink colour in spout and dots is due to the interaction of the oxide in the slip with chrome in the glaze. The piece was fired in oxidation to 1060°C (1940°F).

Photograph: Peter Lee

I have always enjoyed problem solving. Pots have been a source of curious and engaging problems for many years now. I suspect it is because their nature is so multi-faceted. Utility or function is but one aspect and perhaps serves as shorthand for a much longer list: material chemistry, the realm of ideas, formal constitution, social and cultural context, the pot's relationship to the 'fine arts', 'function' as 'idea', the list goes on. I continue to find all of this extremely engaging.

Mark Pharis

Linda Arbuckle (United States)

Seasonal Event Biscuit Jar, h. 23 cm (9 in.), 1999.

Surface: Wax-resisted and stain-painted maiolica glaze. Low-fired earthenware, oxidation.

In the piece illustrated the orange leaf colour was painted on the unfired maiolica glaze. Black lines were drawn to create the images, then the motifs were wax resisted. Food colouring in the wax resist makes it easier to see where the wax has been applied. The white dividing lines were drawn in with wax resist. The yellow ground colour was brushed onto the entire surface (1 part yellow stain to 3 parts gerstley borate by volume). Any dots of yellow that remained on top of the waxed motifs were cleaned off with a damp sponge. Soluble blue colourant (cobalt sulphate dissolved in water, or Chicory Ceradye) was brushed on alternate quadrants, using the waxed white lines to keep the soluble colour from bleeding into the adjacent yellow colour. The soluble blue over the yellow produces a green colour that is dense and uniform. This piece was fired in oxidation to 1100°C (2012°F).

Photograph: Linda Arbuckle

Strong direct form is a foil for active colour and fluid line quality on the surface, rather like having a nutritious meal before indulging in dessert. The surface further explains the form. The surface leaves gather at the bottom of the form to reinforce the small leaf lugs at the bottom and balance the large leaf for the handle on top. The black band at the bottom adds visual weight and sets a tone as a contrast to the bright fall (autumn) colours above. Fall is a bright, lively time of year, very enjoyable, but behind that is the coming of cold, dark winter.

Linda Arbuckle

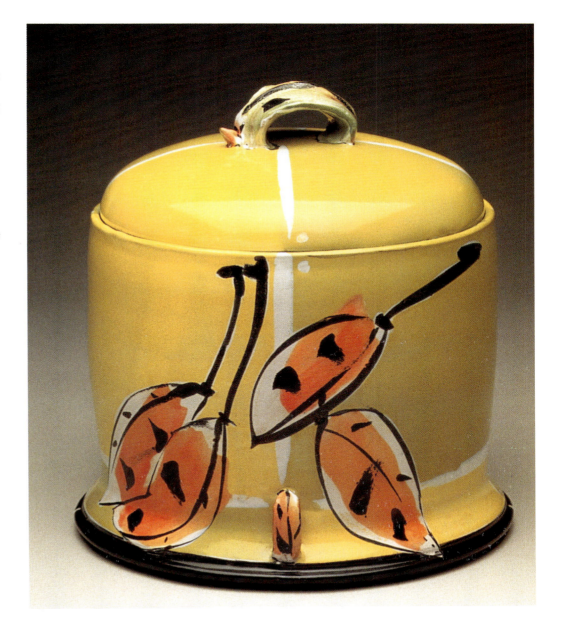

Marc Egan (Canada)

Vase, h. 34 cm (13 ⅜ in.), 2000.

Surface: *Cuerda seca* resist drawing with coloured glaze fill-in. Low-fired earthenware, oxidation.

This vase was wheel-thrown using brown earthenware. After bisquing, the plant outlines were painted on the body using a mixture of wax emulsion and iron oxide. Opaque and coloured transparent glazes were applied by brush in and outside the colour lines. The piece was then electric fired in oxidation to 1140°C (1904°F). The wax lines act as a resist separating colours during application, leaving a dark unglazed line after glaze firing.

Photograph: Marc Egan

I make decorated functional pottery. The imagery reflects my interest in flowers and plants in their natural, representational and abstract forms. I draw inspiration from a variety of sources including Islamic, Southern European and American Arts and Crafts ceramics as well as Japanese and Art Nouveau decorative objects. This work is my interpretation and amalgamation of the above-mentioned sources of inspiration. The cuerda seca technique allows me to work with the interplay of a dry clay line and glaze, glaze colours and textures, and varying opacity/transparency. My aim is to create a sense of movement, tension and depth in the composition in order to strengthen its relationship with the form.

Marc Egan

Jordi Marcet and Rosa Vila-Abadal (Spain)

Back and Front Bowl, w. 56 cm (22 in.), 1997.

Surface: Grease-pencil *cuerda seca* resist with brushed-in colour glazes. High-fired stoneware, oxidation.

This collaborative bowl was wheel-thrown and trimmed, using white stoneware and, once bisqued, had the surface stamped over with stencil pattern lines. These were then outlined with a grease pencil, and coloured feldspathic glazes brushed in by hand. The bowl was gas fired in oxidation to 1260°C (2300°F). Where the resist line burns off, a dark clay line appears and separates all glaze colours.

Photograph: F. Jimenez Bach

Our pieces are the fruit of complete collaboration at all levels – planning, discussing, making and glazing. They can be seen as a reflection of elements, combining ethnology and perhaps a comic expression of industrial design. There is a strong vein of social criticism and ironic thought behind much of our work, a reflection of the concerns of the world we live in.

Jordi Marcet and Rosa Vila-Abadal

Linda Sikora (United States)

Teapot, h. 20 cm (8 in.), w. 20 cm (8 in.), 1999.

Surface: Wax- and latex-resisted polychrome glazes. High-fired porcelain, reduction.

This wheel-thrown porcelain teapot with slab-built spout was bisqued, and a pencil was used to map out a geometric pattern on the surface. A stable black opaque glaze was trailed on, followed by a sideways expanding rutile glaze which softens hard-edged lines. The two were covered with wax, the spout was resisted with latex, and the teapot was dipped in a translucent amber glaze which was also used to line the interior. The latex was removed from the spout, which was glazed in the rutile glaze, and the teapot was fired to 1300°C (2372°F) in a wood- and oil-fuelled salt kiln.

Photograph: Brian Oglesbee

Patterned, glazed porcelain reveals and camouflages the form simultaneously. Whilst rich and sensuous, the glaze also holds a rhythm, logic and structure. The familiar and structural qualities of the decorative pot draw attention to its pragmatic or functional capacity. This may entice one to take it down from the display shelf, where it appears very much in its element, and engage it in use. Made to perform with pleasure both upon viewing and in service, the functional pot positions itself dynamically within a living space. Through imagination and use, it does not come to rest in any one place but continuously stirs.

Linda Sikora

Greg Payce (Canada)

Plate (detail), d. 54 cm (21 ¼ in.), 1994.

Surface: Coloured terra sigillata with latex resist. Low-fired earthenware, oxidation.

This large plate was wheel-thrown and trimmed using red earthenware clay, and patterned with terra sigillata and latex emulsion in the leatherhard state. Fine patterns were painted on by brush, larger shapes (i.e. the heads) were resisted, and more layers of coloured terra sigillata were sprayed on using a mouth atomiser, then further resist was added. Progressive layers of colours were thus built up, and once complete, the latex was removed. The inner border is a 'faux' surface dappled with a rag. The piece was once fired, without polishing, to 1050°C (1922°F) in an electric kiln.

Photograph: Greg Payce

Courtesy of Prime Gallery, Toronto

In my pottery, relationships between forms and images make connections between objects and ideas. I use forms and images generated by myself, recognisable cultural imagery, and hybrids of the two. I set up open-ended relationships between elements in the works. Specific meaning is not necessarily intended. The subjective nature of pottery's unique visual and tactile languages, and its familiar and accessible heritage, facilitate personal readings of the works, distinct from those of other art forms. I am cognisant of my part in a continuing tradition of pottery making, and see my role as one of building and developing the idiom from within it.

Greg Payce

Bente Hansen (Denmark)

Oval Vessel, w. 55 cm (22 in.), 1992.

Surface: Latex-resisted coloured slips on stoneware. High-fired salt glaze, reduction.

This oval vessel was slab constructed by hand from stoneware. After bisquing, areas were carefully resisted with latex resist, sprayed with coloured slips, and resisted and sprayed again. A yellow ball clay/titanium slip overlapping a black slip promotes a green colour under the salt-glaze. The gas kiln was fired up to 1300°C (2372°F), and salting occurred at regular brief intervals as the temperature was descending, over a two-hour period.

Photograph: Ole Akhøj

To me there is an inherent rightness about the use of salt glaze in my work. Although an object may be covered with many layers of slip, the salt merges with the clay, with the form, with the entire object, making it live and breathe in an entirely different way from the usual way of 'normal' glazing – glaze over clay. Salt glazing is very rarely perfect, and that in itself allows for unexpected effects or beauty. To me, the pot is fraught with a deep archetypal meaning, a unique artistic manifestation: a wall of clay enclosing a hollow space and the implied tensions…the hollowness itself, made visible by the opening, and its openness or closure…where the inner can be the opposite of the outer, and yet be intimately connected.

Bente Hansen

Jochen Kuhnhenne (Germany)

Flat Bowl, d. 48 cm (19 in.), 1994.

Surface: Latex-resisted bisque with overall dark matt glaze, added coloured glazes. High-fired stoneware, oxidation.

This shallow bowl was thrown with Westerwald stoneware clay. After bisquing, a pencilled pattern defined those areas to be covered with latex resist, later to become red and white. A black matt feldspathic glaze was sprayed over all, with additional pouring over of a bronze/lithium glaze. When the latex was peeled away, red and white glazes were painted and trailed onto the exposed bisque, and the piece was fired in oxidation to 1260°C (2300°F). Pooling effects occur at the edges of interacting glazes.

Photograph: Holger Phillip

Jochen Kuhnhenne, initially influenced by his teacher Wendelin Stahl, at first experimented with the use of crystalline, crackle and high-viscosity glazes. This led to the complexities of layered resist effects, as well as the use of textured and low-relief surfaces. In the mid-1990s, a few years before his untimely death, his projects included new casting techniques for major oversize vessels and platters; a testimony to a working life of constant development of artistry and skills.

Renate Kuhnhenne

Hans and Birgitte Börjeson (Denmark)

Bowl, h. 20 cm (8 in.), w. 38 cm (15 in.), 2000.

Surface: Paper-resisted coloured slips on stoneware. Once-fired salt-glaze, high-fired, reduction.

Once the bowl was thrown and trimmed, patterns were cut from a layer of bonded paper and tinfoil, and added to the outside surface. The paper side next to the clay absorbs moisture and sticks, the outer foil side provides strength and flexibility. Various coloured slips were sprayed on and patterns were resisted several times for multiple colour effects. After all colours were applied and the piece was dried, it was once fired in a gas kiln in reduction to 1300°C (2372°F), with several saltings beginning at 1250°C (2282°F). Ordinary fine dry kitchen salt was sprayed into the kiln with a sand-blasting gun.

Photograph: Planet

This particular technique provides a unique way of juxtaposing many colours and allowing them to interact at their edges. The overall salt surface provides a natural softening effect to the geometric colour patterning below.

Hans and Birgitte Börjeson

Sophie MacCarthy (United Kingdom)

Trellis Plate, d. 29 cm (11 ¼ in.), 1999.

Surface: Underglaze slip stencils with sgraffito. Low-fired earthenware, oxidation.

After throwing, trimming and drying, this plate was covered with a dark slip base. The dry earthenware absorbs the slip colours easily, and allows for multi-layering of colours and tonal depths. Slip colours were individually mixed, much like a painter's palette, using the base clay as slip, and then coloured with stains and oxides. Addition of water to the slips allows for transparent overlap effects. Paper leaf stencils copied from real leaves, along with areas of wax resist, build up complex colour layers, and finely-scratched sgraffito lines into the clay add details.

Photograph: Stephen Brayne

Most obviously, one of my sources of inspiration is from nature – in this case leaves. I look at fine art, classical and modern, and feel drawn to the works of such artists as Michelangelo, Ingres, Picasso and Matisse. The urban landscape is also an inspiration, particularly East London, with its crumbling, dilapidated buildings, rusty corrugated iron fences, and graffiti-covered walls.

Sophie MacCarthy

Friederike Rahn (Canada)

Persian Cups, d. 8 cm (2 ⅜ in.), h. 8 cm (2 ⅜ in.), 2000.

Surface: Flashing slip with resisted salt-glaze. High-fired stoneware, reduction.

These two cups were wheel-thrown using a porcellaneous stoneware. The leatherhard cups were dipped in a thin flashing slip and subsequently bisqued. Surface patterns were drawn on with a pencil. The left cup was glazed with a light salt glaze, inside and handle, with a trailed glaze pattern on the bottom. The upper half was tape-resisted, and dipped in an iron-saturate glaze. The right cup was resisted with wax over the slip, and dipped in a black glaze. Both pieces were salt fired, in a light reduction to 1300°C (2372°F).

Photograph: Friederike Rahn

I take pleasure in using pots for their tactile and sensuous qualities, and I try to evoke these feelings in my work. My work has changed in the past two years to be more pared down and subtle, with the idea of drawing the viewer into the intimate space of the pot. I am attracted to the idea of plastic decoration, of using fragments of found textures pressed into the soft surfaces of a piece, and of forms built like dresses, sewn together from flat, patterned sheets. Vessel forms present themselves in the landscape of my daily life – the tanker ships in the harbour, a shoe store window, an old kitchen appliance, a detail of construction on a roof.

Friederike Rahn

Patrick Siler (United States) OPPOSITE

Droll Divers, h. 117 cm (46 in.), w. 40.5 cm (16 in.), 1999.

Surface: Paper stencil-resisted engobes. Mid-firing range stoneware, oxidation.

This piece was loosely slab constructed of a coarse mid-firing range stoneware. Once the structure was assembled and in the vertical, a variety of paper stencils, already drawn and cut-out, were selected for application to the piece. Areas to be stencilled were covered with a dark vitreous slip, and the stencil was shifted around to its final position, then lightly wet and attached. A light contrasting slip was brushed over, and loose accent colour slips provide a soft-edged balance to the linear stencil drawings. Once slips were dry, the stencils were removed, and the piece was carefully dried, spray-glazed with a thin transparent wash, and once-fired in oxidation to about 1170°C (2138°F).

Photograph: Patrick Siler

The images I use come from my everyday experiences or just come to me. If certain of these objects and images possess an unusual amount of visual presence and emotive power I try to put them together in a way that feels right by means of a kind of automatic or unconscious association. I like to combine objects that are not ordinarily associated, and objects between which there is potentially an emotional tension. I put imagery on the piece in a way that reflects that tension, conflicts with the form, and possibly suggests that there is more to the image than will fit on the piece.

Patrick Siler

Yasuo Hayashi (Japan)

Prelude 96-B, h. 44 cm (17 ¼ in.), w. 36 cm (14 ¼ in.), 1996.

Surface: Masked coloured engobes and white porcelain inlay. High-fired stoneware, oxidation.

This form was coil constructed using a red and white stoneware with a fine grog. When the shape was fully dry it was sprayed with a red clay using a mouth sprayer (*kirifuki*) and a cut line was inlaid with white porcelain. After an 1100°C (2012°F) firing, specially cut masking tapes were applied as resists and black, brown, red and blue porcelain slips were also sprayed on. Ash glaze was finely sprayed on in three to five successive firing stages, up to 1230°C (2246°F) each.

Photograph: Yasuo Hayashi

Hayashi joined Shiko-Kai, the first avant-garde ceramic group in 1947. He was inspired (like Isamu Noguchi) by a traditional Japanese pattern known as 'chokkomon' (a crossing of straight lines and arcs, Kofun period, 4–6 BC). Hayashi's intellectual pursuit of pure forms to the utmost limit has more in common with Picasso, Cézanne and Mondrian than the popular Japanese taste for 'yohen' and penchant for deformation. His rejection of the 'immature' (in his eyes a lack of skill), interpreted as 'honest' or 'natural' as a popular concept in Japanese art, is because he believes viewers actually appreciate their own emotional narcissism. Hayashi has always been carefully to avoid such narcissism in both art and life. He was the first truly avant-garde Japanese ceramic artist. A forerunner to Kazuo Yagi (to whom this place is usually attributed), his true place in post-war Japanese ceramics has only recently been acknowledged.

Excerpt from *The Path of the Space of Optical Illusions* by Shigenobu Kimura,
Translation courtesy of Dorothy Feibleman

Sara Carone (Brazil)

Plate, d. 28.5 cm (11 ¼ in.), 1991.

Surface: Resist patterns with adhesive splice tapes and slip and glaze masking. Low-fired, raku, oxidation.

This plate was thrown using a low-fire raku clay and, once burnished, was carefully bisqued in a reducing atmosphere to establish various surface tonalities. Thin auto-adhesive splice tapes (used normally for design layout of printed circuit boards) were added in a controlled linear pattern, and the overall surface was coated with first a kaolin/water mixture, and then an alkaline frit. Their combined and controlled thickness determines subsequent crackle and dot patterns, as well as halo effects. After studied placing in the raku kiln in order to promote varied surface effects, the piece was slowly fired to 850°C (1562°F) and once cooled to 520°C (968°F), bags of sawdust were carefully inserted. After cooling, the masking glazes were removed to reveal subtle colour effects, and black lines where the splice tapes were applied.

Photograph: Romulo Fialdini

Before working in ceramics, I drew, painted and made etchings and metal sculpture, and was drawn to Post-Impressionist painting and early 20th-century movements such as fauvism, cubism and expressionism. My work in ceramics does not aspire to functionalism, but rather to the making of objects of pure form in a personal idiom.

Sara Carone

chapter eight
Third-firing on-glaze techniques

Third-firing on-glaze techniques involve the application of pattern and imagery to an already glaze-fired surface. First firing is usually bisque, second firing is usually glaze, third firing is 'on-glaze'. There are three distinct categories here, with some combination overlaps. The first is the use of low-fired lustres (metallic compounds such as gold, silver, copper and platinum) fused to the glaze-fired surface, in oxidation or reduction. Lustre resist and lustre sgraffito can be used here. The second category deals with overglaze (on-glaze) enamels or china paints, which fuse onto rather than into the glaze, usually at around 750°C (1382°F) in oxidation. Although made from the usual ceramic colouring oxides, they resemble more oil- or emulsion-based paints, leave a slightly raised surface, and provide a brighter, broader colour palette than normal high-firing stains and oxides. The last category deals with transfers (decals), designed or photo images printed in oil-based ceramic inks onto specially gummed varnished paper. The 'plastic' image is soaked off and arranged on the glaze-fired surface, where it is low-fired and fused on. All these techniques can be used in conjunction with one another, but usually require separate successive firings.

Dalia Laučkaitė-Jakimavičienė (Lithuania)

Farewell Plate, d. 33 cm (13 in.), 1998.

Surface: Multiple decals and fine-line enamel detail. Porcelain, low-fired, oxidation.

This industrially-manufactured glazed porcelain plate was used as a base for complex imagery composed of 40–50 small pieces of decals, with added brushed and fine pen line overglaze enamel details. The plate was fired several times in oxidation to 750°C (1382°F).

Photograph: Vidmantas Ilčiukas

I like my pieces to be a bit funny and full of various allusions – personal, historical, religious, mythical. I cut transfers and combine them into solemn, elaborate compositions, telling odd, allegorical, slightly surrealistic stories. My favourite personages are women-birds, sometimes divine as angels, sometimes naughty or even brutal as harpies.

Dalia Laučkaitė-Jakimavičienė

Liz Quackenbush
(United States)

Oval Insect Platter, d. 56 cm (22 in.), 2000.

Surface: Maiolica with copper and cobalt in-glaze painting and gold lustre.
Low-fired earthenware, oxidation.

This press-moulded terracotta platter with a coiled rim was bisqued and glazed with a white (maiolica) tin glaze. Patterns were painted in-glaze using cobalt and copper carbonate, and the piece was fired in oxidation to 1080°C (1976°F). After glaze firing, gold lustre was painted over the background and the platter was refired in oxidation to 750°C (1382°F).

Photograph: Dick Ackley

I first became aware of lustreware with Iranian pieces that activated the clay surface and celebrated their own history of metal form and surface. As time passed I also became inspired by other approaches to lustre, and I have worked to exploit its many visual illusions. Sometimes it looks dirty, creating the illusion of a polluted atmosphere. I first saw this happen in Staffordshire cobalt-silver lustre painting. At other times lustre simply acts as a beautiful yellow-gold background colour. This approach was used in Deruta and Gubbio in Italy in the 1500s. I have found myself using lustre in all of these ways. I realise I am investigating a visual language that has entertained pottery decorators for a long time. I am happy to be a part of this longstanding pottery tradition.

Liz Quackenbush

Joan Takayama-Ogawa (United States) OPPOSITE

Chrysanthemum Bowl, h. 33 cm (13 in.), w 25.5 cm (10 in.), 1992

Surface: Slip nodules, underglazes with transparent glaze, gold lustre. Low-fired earthenware, oxidation

This piece was thrown and assembled using a low-fired mineral ceramics porcelain. The same clay in slip form was applied (using a Catsup/ketchup bottle) to create surface nodules at the greenware stage. Underglazes and a transparent lead glaze were aplied after bisquing, and the piece was fired to 1060°C (1940°F), followed by a gold lustre application and two firings to 680°C (1256°F).

Photograph: Anthony Cuñha
Courtesy of Ferrin Gallery,
Lenox, Massachusetts

Seeing Louis Comfort Tiffany's clay vases, in which he incorporated botanical imagery into the form, inspired Chrysanthemum Bowl. *This piece was brought to birth dangerously. During the wheel-throwing process, the wide flange can slump and warp. The edge of the flange and the surface are carved, and cracking is a real issue. The applied slip must be applied at the right time or warping will occur. The piece is fired four times: bisque, glaze, gold (twice). Each firing is a hazard. When I opened the kiln and saw* Chrysanthemum Bowl *in its finished form, it was better than opening presents on Christmas morning.*

Joan Takayama-Ogawa

Paul Mathieu (Canada)

Tulip Vase, h. 25 cm (9 ⅞ in.), 1996.

Surface: Lustre resist with metallic lustre. Thrown and altered porcelain, low-fired, oxidation.

This porcelain shape was thrown on the wheel, and while still malleable, disrupted by creating arbitrary bumps and depressions, both in and outside. After bisquing, the piece was glazed with a dark marine blue glaze and fired twice to 1260°C (2300°F). Using a fine brush and lustre resist the figure outlines were painted on, loosely creating imagery of body parts over the arbitrary surface distortions. Each figure was then painted with metallic lustre, using gold, bronze and copper, in bright matt. After low firing to 750°C (1382°F), the lustre resist was brushed off, to reveal a dark glaze outline.

Photograph: Kumiko Yasukawa
Courtesy of Prime Gallery, Toronto

The 'trick' and fun of this erotic piece is to match the intertwined body parts with the bumps and depressions created arbitrarily previously. The varying lustres create a richly baroque surface, which still suggestively defines individual forms within the tangled mass. In the end it isn't how one does anything that matters, it is what one does and why that counts.

Paul Mathieu

Julia Galloway (United States)

Salt, Pepper, Oil, Vinegar, 10 x 15 x 24 cm (4 x 6 x 9 ½ in.), 2000.

Surface: Textured lustre over trailed glaze, soda-fired porcelain. Mid-firing range, oxidation.

This functional set was made of thrown and altered porcelain, with the double spouts serving to intertwine poured oil and vinegar. The pots were covered with flashing slip and then bisqued. Lids were trailed with glaze for texture, and vessels' sides were resisted in lozenge shapes and glazed with copper glaze. After soda firing in a gas kiln to 1190°C (2176°F), lids were lustred over the raised patterned glaze and the set was fired in oxidation to 715°C (1319°F). The tray was made of slabbed, altered and pierced raw fire clay, fired in oxidation to 1190°C (2174°F).

Photograph: Julia Galloway

I am interested in pottery that is joyous; objects that weave into our daily lives through use, pots that decorate our living spaces with character and elegance. In making sets, I am curious about their own inherent dialogue; the set itself is reminiscent of close conversations, and their ritual celebratory use. My colour palette is influenced by my interest in historical Persian miniature paintings, prints and textiles. For form inspiration I look closely at historical Chinese ceramics, (specifically Sung and Tang) and the European porcelains (specifically Sèvres and Meissen). I am also extremely influenced by many potters and artists including Betty Woodman, Sarah Coote, Walter Ostrom, Martin Puryear, and Antoinette Rosato.

Julia Galloway

Alan Caiger-Smith
(United Kingdom)

Bowl, w. 45 cm (17 ¾ in.), 2000.

Surface: Reduced lustre pigments on tin glaze. Low-fired earthenware, oxidation.

This bowl was wheel-thrown and trimmed, using red earthenware clay. After electric bisquing to 1010°C (1850°F), it was glazed with a tin glaze, and again electric fired to 1050°C (1922°F). The white-glazed surface was freely decorated by brush, using hand-prepared silver and copper compound pigments, mixed with natural red ochre from Devonshire. The pigments were lightly calcified and ground in a jar mill for two hours. The bowl was refired in a wood kiln over an eight- to nine- hour period to about 650°C (1202°F), with clear burning periods between a number of small reductions toward the end of the firing cycle.

Photograph: Hilary Manser
Collection of Liam and Bernardine Hudson

Much of my painting on pots is a kind of dance with the brush. The form is static. The brush moves, making calligraphic lines, rhythms and spaces, stillness and movement combined, 'a world within a world'. This applies to any pigment one uses, but lustre enhances the movement by reflecting light. In the wood-fired kiln certain pigments produce vapouring around the brushstrokes and in the surrounding glaze. This is very different from clear-cut 'classic' lustre, but I encourage it to happen. It integrates the design with the form as a whole.

Alan Caiger-Smith

Ralph Bacerra (United States) OPPOSITE

Lidded Celadon Vessel, h. 63.5 cm (25 in.), w. 44.5 cm (18 ¼ in.), 1999.

Surface: Lustres and overglaze enamels over celadon glaze. Low-fired, oxidation.

This lidded vessel was slab constructed using porcelain clay. Once bisque fired, the piece was spray glazed and brushed with a celadon glaze, and gas fired in reduction to 1330°C (2426°F). Details were painted on-glaze with overglaze enamels and gold lustre, using a variety of fine brushes, and the vessel was refired in oxidation to 760°C (1400°F).

Photograph: Anthony Cuñha
Courtesy of Frank Lloyd Gallery,
Santa Monica, CA

Unapologetically a decorative artist, Bacerra's muses were the potters who centuries ago decorated the Japanese palace wares of Kutani, Nabeshima and Imari, with their masterful use of surface decoration, often inspired by the pattern on fabric design. His fine arts' affinities tend towards optical systems and stylisation, a mix of M.C. Escher (without his mechanistic elements), with a dash of Warhol. The work also reflects the man, one who has a paper-thin tolerance for any form of pretension. So his pots have no secret meanings. They carry no messages. They are not deconstructivist except accidentally so in the kiln. They are not laden with symbol metaphor or irony. They celebrate thousands of years of decorative pottery and yet, even though they are not instruments of intellectual inquiry, they are intelligent objects alive with visual acuity.

From: *Ralph Bacerra: A Survey* by Garth Clark

Sutton Taylor (United Kingdom)

Vase, h. 59 cm (23 in.), w. 39 cm (15 ½ in.), 2000.

Surface: Multiple-fired slips, glazes and lustres. High-fired porcelain, reduction.

This vase was slab-constructed from a self-prepared fine stoneware-frit body. After an oxidation bisque firing, three more firings took place. The second, at 1000°C (1832°F), hardened underglaze slips containing various metal salts (gold, silver or copper) that catalysed subsequent glaze layers. The third high-firing (up to 1260°C/2300°F) melted a transparent glaze layer. The fourth firing was for pigment lustres, in the form of a clay paste (with up to 25% metal) which was painted on the fired glaze and fired in strong gas-reduction to 750°C (1382°F) in order to leave a film of pure metal or colour absorbed onto and into the glaze. After cooling, the clay residue was scraped away.

Photograph: Richard Littlewood
Courtesy of Hart Gallery, London

My work is concerned with the use of colour as a vehicle of expression and a means of evoking emotional and spiritual responses, as well as with the abstract depiction of situations observed in the natural work which have caused delight. I am attracted to bright and changing light conditions in expansive skies and moving water – to light through foliage – to patterns and juxtapositions of colour in the landscape – to patterns of light and shade in rock faces or in individual pebbles. Any one of a million remembered images may be the starting point for a pot, but once begun, a valid piece will take on its own life and dictate what it requires to become itself – and this is the enduring fascination.

Sutton Taylor

Yuriko Matsuda (Japan) OPPOSITE

Calabash with Polka Dot, h. 30 cm (11 ¾ in.), 1998.

Surface: Overglaze enamels on porcelain. Low-fired, oxidation.

This calabash shape was made with porcelain slab strips draped and scraped over a plaster mould, with visible joining marks. After bisquing, the shape was glazed with a transparent glaze outside, and a black glaze inside (with visible exterior drip marks), and gas fired in reduction to 1260°C (2300°F). Overall decoration was completed with painted overglaze enamels, and the piece was electric fired to 740°C (1364°F).

Photograph: T. Iwasaki
Courtesy of Gallery Dai Ichi Arts Ltd, New York

In the world of art today, we are inundated with information which shrinks the barriers of time and space, where East meets West and past meets present. It seems almost impossible to create work without being influenced by this in some way. Based on this realisation, I create homages to, and parodies of, historically renowned works; here a banal vegetable shape is painted with contemporary dots and stripes, using a technique that dates back to the Ming dynasty.

Yuriko Matsuda

Susan Thayer (United States)

Farewell Florida, h. 24 cm (9 ½ in.), w. 34.5 cm (13 ⅝ in.), 1999.
Surface: Multi-fired china paints on porcelain. Low-fired, oxidation.

This piece was made of assembled castings in porcelain slip, refined through surface carving, with added three-dimensional elements sculpted from porcelain slip. After bisquing and glazing, some underglaze colouring took place. After a porcelain glaze firing, detailed imagery was china-painted on-glaze, and built up over a series of firings (sometimes as many as 20) to 700°C (1292°F).

Photograph: Dean Reynolds
Courtesy of Ferrin Gallery, Lenox, Massachusetts

These forms are vessels, their contents and stories sometimes mysterious. I invite the viewer to freely interpret these scenes, creating a narrative, as in a dream. Although no longer functional in the literal sense, my teapots retain their association with the participatory event of taking tea. I begin each piece in recognition of an opportunity to realise a vision. Because ceramic materials touch our lives daily in innumerable ways, they have an intrinsic ability to provoke response. My work draws upon that familiarity, augmented by a vocabulary of images and terms derived from the history of ceramic vessels, to participate in the evolution of the tradition of ideas expressed through objects.

Susan Thayer

Jane Osborn-Smith (United States)

Metamorphosis, h. 17.8 cm (7 in.), w. 12.7 cm (5 in.), 2000.

Surface: Multiple-fired matt enamels on porcelain. High-fired, oxidation.

This vessel form was made from slipcast porcelain, using a mould taken from a shaped piece of clay. The casting allows for walls of eggshell-like thinness, which were delicately carved before firing to translucency at 1260°C (2300°F). They were then sanded and burnished, and painted with enamels over several colour firings, between 710°C (1310°F) and 780°C (1436°F), in oxidation.

Photograph: Peter Aldridge

Courtesy of Ferrin Gallery, Lenox, Massachusetts

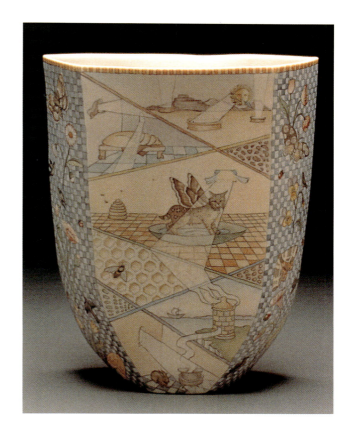

Each pot takes a long time to complete and during this time I feel as if I inhabit it much as a mollusc inhabits its shell. The paintings therefore express my thoughts and preoccupations during this period. Some pieces are emotive, others narrative. As I vacate each vessel and move on to the next, I leave them as containers for others to interpret the forms and imagery in the light of their own experiences.

Jane Osborn-Smith

Maruta Raude (Latvia)

My Lovely Teapot (detail), h. 21 cm (8 ¼ in.), 2000.

Surface: Overglaze enamels and lustres on porcelain. Low-fired, oxidation.

For some years my work theme has been garden. Garden as a symbol – a paradise garden, the primary garden, as a place where nature is tamed, arranged, selected and encircled. Garden – as opposed to the unconsciousness of the forest. My garden is full of trees, plants and birds. There are some items left there by humans – half-empty teacups, some picked fruits on the table. Sometimes there are ladders in the garden, which symbolise spirituality and eagerness to rise. My work is influenced by various periods and artists. I can mention Egyptian paintings here as well as the artists Matisse and Hundertwasser.

Maruta Raude

This teapot was slipcast in a self-made plaster mould using a commercial white porcelain clay with added sodium silicate for ease of casting. Once bisqued to 900°C (1652°F), it was glazed in a transparent leadless glaze and electric-fired to 1300°C (2300°F). Black on-glaze pigment mixed with sugar and water and applied with a stylus created black outlines, which were filled in with enamels, followed by scratched-through details. Colour areas were recoated with thin, semi-transparent enamels and other unpainted areas were painted with gold and white lustres. The piece was fired in oxidation to 750°C (1382°F).

Photograph: Aigars Jukna

Kurt Weiser (United States) OPPOSITE

Perfume, h. 48 cm (19 in.), w. 30.5 cm (12 in.), 2000.

Surface: Porcelain with multi-fired overglaze enamels. High-fired, oxidation.

This vessel was made of slipcast porcelain with added handbuilt components. After bisquing, a clear glaze was poured over, and the piece was fired to 1250°C (2282°F). All details painted were done with overglaze enamels, using brushes or a pounce (a cotton pad covered with silk). The piece was refired to 700°C (1292°F), repainted and refired with as many as five firings for colour, depth and richness.

Photograph: Kurt Weiser

For years the work I did in ceramics was about ceramics. As interesting as this was to me I always had a vague feeling that the best expression of the nature of ceramics only came as a gift of nature. Somewhere in the middle of all this I realised that the materials are there to allow you to say what you want to say, not to tell you what to say. So I gave up trying to control nature and decided to just try and say what I thought about it.

Kurt Weiser

Cindy Kolodziejski (United States)

Clapping Monkey, h. 28 cm (11 in.), 2000.

Surface: Computer-manipulated image painted in underglazes, glazes and china paints. Low-fired earthenware, oxidation.

This shape was made from slipcast earthenware components, depicting a reflected image in a silver pitcher, copied onto a silver-pitcher shape. The computer-manipulated image was printed onto paper and transferred directly onto the bisqued pitcher shape. Hand painting with underglazes was followed by the application of transparent glaze and glaze colour washes, with matt black glaze applied to the handle. After electric firing to 1000°C (1832°F), the piece was enhanced by the addition of complex layers of china paint with multiple low-firings up to 720°C (1328°F).

Photograph: Anthony Cuñha
Courtesy of Garth Clark Gallery, New York

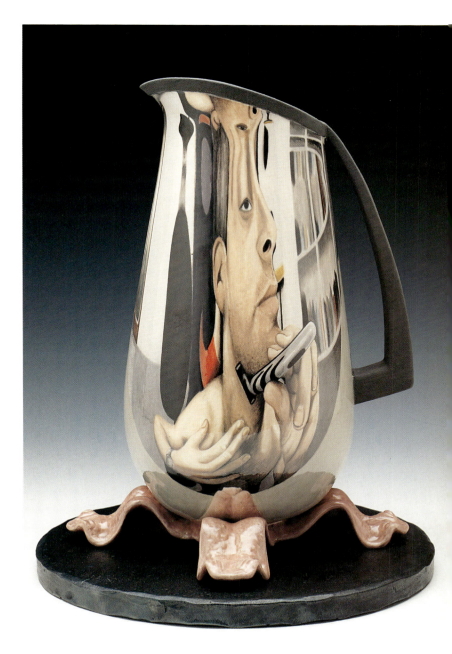

My work is an attempt at bending the boundaries of Western decorative arts, ceramic tradition painting and good taste for the purpose of inducing complex narratives. Some of the conventions I play with include the various periods of Western Art from classical to baroque to modern. While I see value in violating conventions, doing so in the service of psychological narratives is the essence of my work. My medium exists between painting and ceramics, aiming at a kind of conceptual drama. I work with composite forms, found images, and implied narratives. My recent work pushes my forms into areas of vertiginous distortion matched only by the forking paths of my imagery, which range from mortality to sexuality.

Cindy Kolodziejski

Juris Bergens (Latvia)

Teapot: Self-Portrait with Grandfathers, 25 x 25 cm (9 ⅞ x 9 ⅞ in.), 1997.

Surface: Handpainted china paints. Bone china, low-fired, oxidation.

This complex piece was assembled from slipcast bone china sections cast from plaster moulds and wood. After bisquing and coating with a transparent glaze, the piece was electric fired to 1100°C (2012°F). All images were painted by hand with china paints copying photo imagery (no transfers), using brush, sponge and needle. Lustre details and solid colour enamels were added and the piece was refired to 750°C (1382°F).

Photograph: Aigars Jukna

I use ceramics as a three-dimensional canvas to express my feelings about social situations and my own life. In this instance I am referring to the political changes in the former Soviet block, post 1987. Symbology is personal here: a banana skin, a cross, a bent screw, family photos – a record of times past and the remnants of broken dreams and aspirations.

Juris Bergens

James Klueg (United States)

Dictum, h. 33 cm (13 in.), w. 23 cm (9 in.), 1999.

Surface: Transparent glaze, on-glaze black stain and sgraffito refired. Low-fired earthenware, oxidation.

After slab-construction from a light-coloured earthenware, this piece was bisqued to 1100°C (2012°F), glazed inside with a liner glaze and outside with a clear glaze, and again fired to 1100°C (2012°F). Several coats of black stain were brushed on the entire piece and all texts and imagery sgraffitoed. A final electric firing took place, again at 1100°C (2012°F).

Photograph: James Klueg

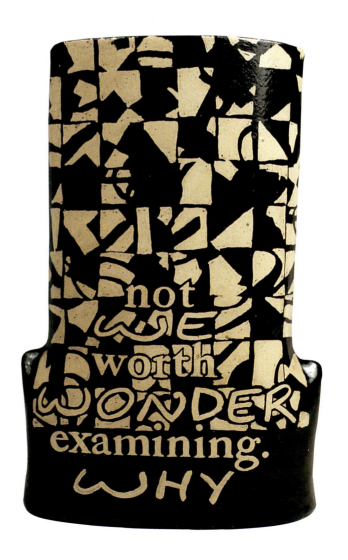

Pots are, for me, domestically scaled visual objects, perfect for the kinds of things I wish to suggest. Very simply, I think I'm making art pottery that reflects my version of our personal and impersonal world. In the studio, I thrive on the integration of idea and technique; like the chicken and egg, I'm never sure which comes first. I'm probably more than mildly obsessive about surface enhancement, to the point where elaborate means I frequently produce offhand effects. I like to disappear behind style. I especially relish the irony of doing things by hand that most professionals relegated to a computer a long time ago. Viva inefficiency!

James Klueg

Bodil Manz (Denmark)

Oval Form Decorated with Black, h. 22 cm (8 ⅝ in.), w. 31 cm (12 ¼ in.), 2000.

Surface: High-fired screenprint transfers. Porcelain, oxidation.

This oval cylinder form was made of slipcast porcelain, which, after bisquing, was reheated in order to absorb a sprayed white matt feldspathic glaze on very thin clay walls. The piece was then fired in oxidation to 1300°C (2372°F). Geometric patterns were drawn on paper, sent to a professional screenprinter, and made into transfers. These were then cut and applied to the outside in precise patterns, and the piece was fired again to 1300°C (2372°F).

Photograph: Ole Ackøj

I work very often with simple lines, both thick and thin, with consideration of the spaces between those lines – a balance of light and dark. Small things around me, as well as landscapes, can inspire me, but I return again and again to a kind of minimal abstraction, and ongoing research into the simplest possible patterning, that nonetheless remains profound for me; a paring down of ideas into essential elements.

Bodil Manz

Angelo di Petta (Canada)

Valle, 41 x 24 cm (16 x 9 ½ in.), 2000.

Surface: Screen- and block-printed decals on maiolica (tin glaze). Low-fired earthenware, oxidation.

This piece was slipcast from a plaster mould made from a solid template-shaped piece of clay. Once dried, the exterior was coated with red terra sigillata, and once bisqued to 1100°C (2012°F), commercial maiolica glaze was brushed on the inside, sprayed with charcoal fixative to 'harden' the glaze, and brushed with several washes of stain. After glaze firing in oxidation to 1040°C (1904°F), two types of transfers were applied: the first using imagery screened onto gummed transfer paper, the second using graphite rubbings from carved plaster slabs, applied to the paper using a serrated blade, and block prints, with an oil-based medium and copper carbonate. Once dry, the piece was fired to 1000°C (1832°F), and the procedure was repeated several times.

Photograph: Wayne Eardley

Generally, my work has been guided less by the need to 'decorate' a form and more by the desire to arrive at a natural 'decoration' which is the result of a process. Valle is the Italian word for valley. A valley is a topographical 'container'. One stands at the edge of a valley and looks into it as one would look into a bowl. The physical analogy between valley and bowl becomes obvious. Valle is a generalisation, expressed in clay, of the form which makes up the landscape. The imagery does not represent anything in particular but should be considered as an investigation of natural occurrences seen up close and at a distance. The Italian title links with the technique used here (maiolica), an oblique reference to the historical and artistic development of maiolica which took place in Italy during the Renaissance.

Angelo di Petta

Richard Slee (United Kingdom)

Pod Dish, 68 cm (26 ¼ in.), 2000.

Surface: On-glaze print transfer. Low-fired earthenware, oxidation.

This dish was handbuilt with an added extruded rim, using a formulated light earthenware body. After bisquing, commercial low-solubility coloured glazes were applied, and the piece was fired to 1080°C (1976°F). Computer artwork (prepared through Mac PhotoShop) was sent to a commercial printer to produce an on-glaze transfer print. This was applied to the glazed surface and refired in oxidation to 1080°C (1976°F), with a 45-minute soak.

Photograph: Richard Slee

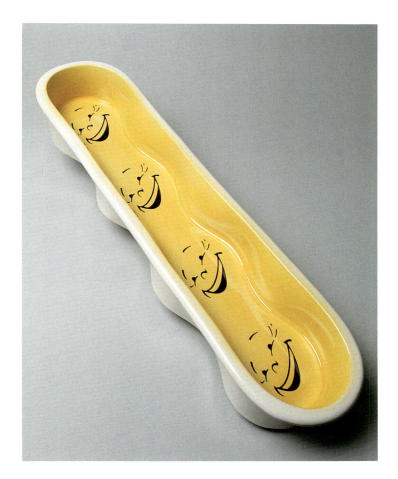

The plates I make are sourced from the fast-disappearing common canteen of earthenware crockery; heavy, cheap and fat. But they do possess the nobler proportions of European chargers or that of old pewter ware. Decoration – I avoid the word as being too gentle. In this instance, the 'happy face' pastiche, borrowed form computer clip art, becomes meaningful as contemporary iconography, with recognizable pop art roots. Technique is hidden, a use of mechanical screenprint and shiny glaze to produce a contradiction between the handmade and the industrial.

Richard Slee

Paul Scott (United Kingdom)

The Scott Collection, Cumbrian Blue(s)/ Seascape Pigeon No. 5, w. 44 cm, 2000.

Surface: Digitally-manipulated and collaged transfer image. Low-fired bone china, oxidation.

This appropriated glazed bone china plate was used as a background for a transfer image. The imagery was drawn on an Apple computer, collaging old engravings and digitally-altered photographs to create a contemporary landscape pattern, and was then screenprinted in ceramic underglaze colour and made into transfers. These were collaged onto the glazed surface and fired to 1100°C (2012°F). Gold lustre was applied to the rim, and the plate was refired to 750°C (1382°F).

Photograph: Paul Scott

I have always been interested in painting, printmaking and drawing. Over the years I have developed most of my work in a ceramic medium. Drawing (on paper and in notebooks) has never really left me though, and now I find myself increasingly drawn to digital image manipulation which is used in my printed and collaged work. This plate is a tribute to, and a subversion of, the Blue and White genre of industrially-produced pottery. In place of the fantasy landscapes, my work commemorates the real (nuclear and industrial) landscapes of late 20th-century England.

Paul Scott

Daniel Kruger
(Germany)

Embracing Couple Vase, h. 27.5 cm (10 ⅞ in.), w. 18 cm (7 ⅛ in.), 1997. Made at the European Ceramics Work Centre, Netherlands

Surface: Slipcast porcelain with surface embellishments, photo transfer and gold lustre. High-fired, oxidation.

The vase form was made of slipcast porcelain, with added moulded rock- and leaf-shaped embellishments. After glaze firing in oxidation to 1260°C (2300°F), a photo transfer image was added. These transfer images were printed onto a gelatine film which was backed with paper. On moistening the paper, the gelatine film with the image was released and transferred onto the fired glaze surface. Gold lustre was added to the foot, and the piece was refired to 750°C (1382°F).

Photograph: Peer van der Kruis

My subject matter is about concerns I have and believe I share with many other people. It deals with homo-eroticism but not in an exclusively gay context: the male figure and the sensuality it conveys is apparent in many cultures and periods, taking on varied forms to express its many aspects. Tender interactions between men can, but do not necessarily, have an erotic component. I hope to show more than just the physical aspect of masculinity, and go beyond the erotic-sensual.

Daniel Kruger

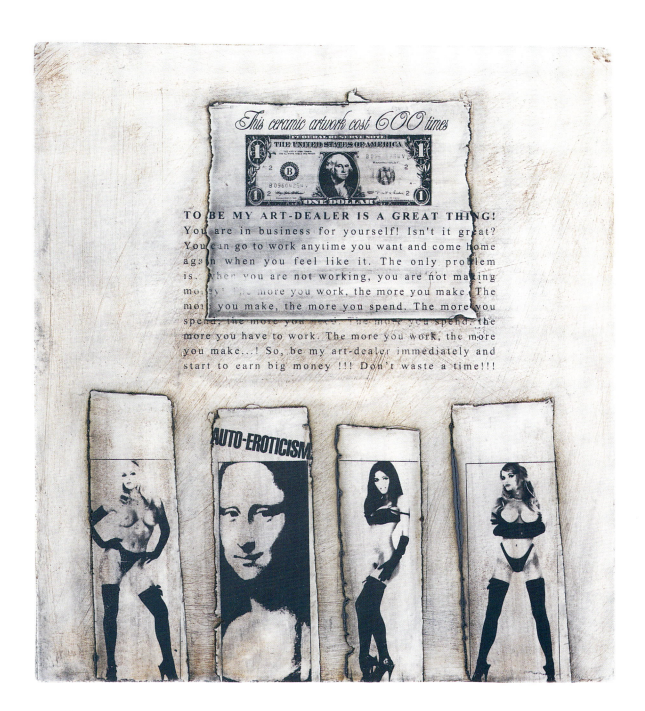

Thomas Sipavicius (Hungary)

Who Wants to be My Art Dealer II?, 34 x 35 cm (13 ⅜ x 13 ¾ in.), 2000.

Surface: Direct photo-emulsion printing on porcelain paper clay. High-fired, oxidation.

This piece was produced much in the way a regular photograph is printed. A porcelain paper clay sheet was covered with transparent glaze and electric-fired to 1300°C (2372°F). Computer-manipulated imagery in the form of positive, real-size offset film was printed in a darkroom onto the glazed porcelain surface, made light sensitive in advance, using photographic emulsion containing ammonium bichromate. After exposure, the piece was developed with powdered underglaze pigments and fired to 1180°C (2156°F).

Photograph: Zoltan Csiko

This work is part of a series of 25 pieces based on Andy Warhol's proclamation 'Everybody could be famous for at least 15 minutes'. It is a comment on society, the price paid for social-climbing and celebrity, what I call our 'social disease', the false cheek-kissing, the climbing to the top, the artist seeking fame through the art dealer, etc., etc.

Thomas Sipavicius

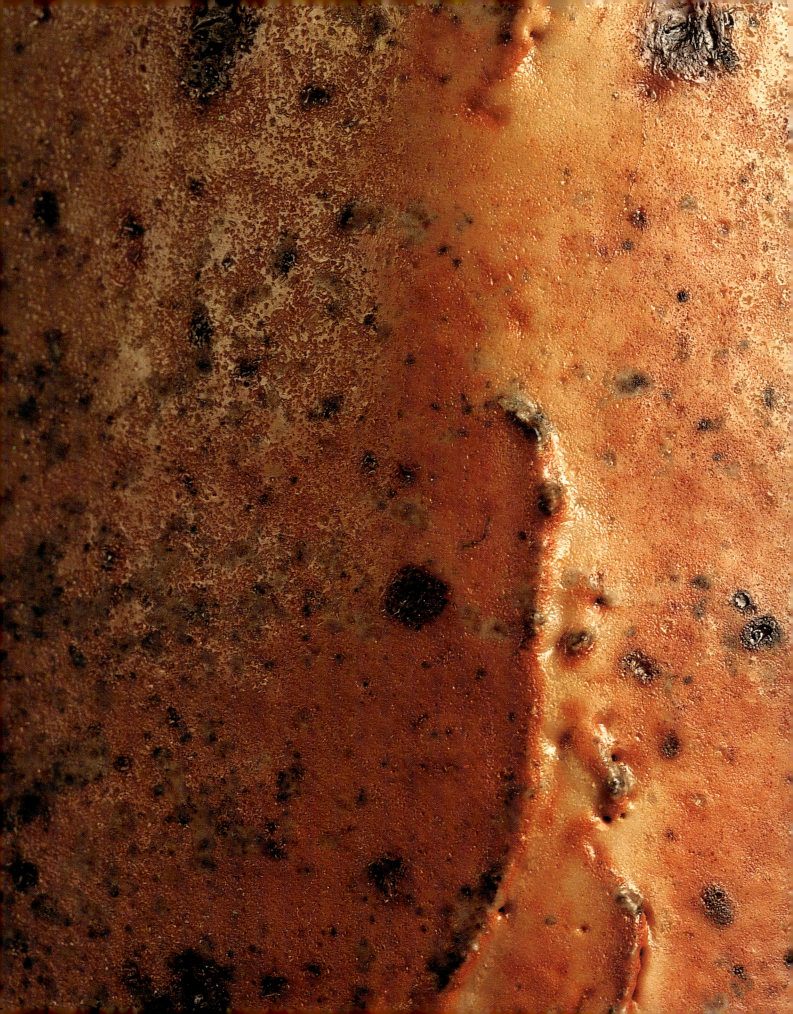

chapter nine

Fire, smoke and ash surfaces

Fire, Smoke and Ash Surfaces depend for their primary visual impact on flashing marks from flames, surface smoke effects from heavy reduction, and glaze and slip surfaces reacting in general to the passage of flames and smoke in a fuel-fired kiln. Included here are works that are wood-fired in *Anagama* kilns and Bourry-box kilns at high temperatures, both glazed and unglazed, and low-fire raku and pit-fire techniques that include the use of terra sigillata and glazes, as well as unglazed surfaces. Salt- and soda-glazed surfaces will have appeared in previous chapters, as they tend to be used more in conjunction with other surface decoration techniques.

Roswitha Wulff (Australia)

Tanami, h. 22 cm (8 ⅝ in.), 1993.

Surface: Wood-fired Shino-type clay/feldspar slip. High-fired stoneware, reduction.

This container shape was made of wheel-thrown stoneware, and covered with a Shino-type clay/feldspar slip. It was wood fired near the firebox in a Bourry-box kiln to over 1300°C. (2372°F) Surface markings are due to slip thickness, flame flashing and fly ash in the kiln.

Photograph: Roswitha Wulff

This piece is inspired by the Tanami Desert of central Australia, an evocation of the pervasive red landscape colours that impressed me profoundly on my travels there.

Roswitha Wulff

Daphne Corregan (France)

Pichets, h. 51 cm (20 in.), w. 25 cm (9 ⅝ in.), 1999.

Surface: Smoked raku-fired slips and glazes. Low-fired earthenware, reduction.

These 'jugs' were slab and coil-constructed of white raku earthenware with a high talc content, with added linear incisions to frame specific colour fields. Coloured slips and boracic glazes were brushed on, and the pieces were fired in a raku fibre kiln to 1050°C (1922°F), in a heavily smoked atmosphere. Pieces were not removed for combustible reduction, but were left to cool in the kiln.

Photograph: Daphne Corregan

I admire the freshness and simplicity of certain kinds of traditional functional wares (i.e. Japanese, Korean and African) as embodied in the contemporary works of such French artists as Brigitte Penichaud, J.N. Gerard, Claude Varlan and Hervé Rousseau. Other artists whose works are inspirational are Cy Twombly, Miquel Barcéló and Picasso (to name a few) expressing simple narratives or visual abstraction in their chosen medium. I often aim for a 'double lecture' (double reading) in my work, a reflection of our society and its relationships.

Daphne Corregan

John Wheeldon
(United Kingdom)

Neolithic Form, h. 23 cm (9 in.), w. 16 cm (6 ¼ in.), 2000.

Surface: Raku-fired copper matt glaze. Low-fired stoneware, oxidation.

This pot was thrown using a white stoneware body grogged with Molochite, and using ribs to ensure a smooth surface. After turning, a thick slip was trailed onto the top few centimetres of the form becoming, after firing, an unglazed, carbonised band. After bisque firing to 980°C (1796°F), a copper matt glaze was applied prior to raku firing, which took place in a small top-loading gas kiln, to around 1000°C (1832°F). The pot was removed with tongs and placed on a thin layer of sawdust, which burned and enveloped it in flames. After a short period of burning it was covered with a metal can and allowed to cool. The resulting colours appear to be a product of the path of the flames during burning, coupled with the reduction period.

Photograph: Rob Wheeldon

My involvement with raku developed from a need to escape from the limitations of the lustre techniques I had previously used, coupled with a desire to use real fire and become more involved with the processes of firing. The transition was made easier as I saw raku as a form of matt, coloured lustre, not a complete break from my earlier work but a complement to it. The forms of much of my work refer to pieces from prehistory, especially the Bronze Age, and have developed from an ancient pot seen in a museum many years ago. I also have a collection of shards found in gardens and fields which span a period from Roman times to the 19th century, and the marks left by the potters are so eloquent (we leave the same marks on our own work today) – it is like a language left by potters to be read by potters. I hope to add a few more words to the vocabulary.

John Wheeldon

Jane Perryman
(United Kingdom)

Burnished Vessel, w. 18 cm (7 in.), 1999.

Surface: Smoke-fired, paper, wax and slip-resisted burnished surface. Low-fired porcelain, reduction.

This vessel form was handbuilt from a mixture of T-material and porcelain clay, using coiling and scraping techniques; it was covered in porcelain slip before bisquing to 970°C (1778°F). A pattern was built up using a combination of wax, paper and slip resists, which burned off at different times during the subsequent smoke firing, creating variegated surfaces. Firing took place in a metal drum container, using dried dung, sawdust and paper as combustibles. After cooling, the piece was cleaned of resist remnants and polished with beeswax.

Photograph: Graham Murrell

Perhaps as a reaction against the increasing sophistication surrounding kiln technology, there is a growing awareness and interest in the traditional techniques of handbuilding and smoke firing which are still being used in countries of low and developing technology. For the last 12 years I have been using the vessel form as a main vehicle of expression; the universal symbol for containing and offering, whether as nourishment for the body or soul. The essence of my work lies in combining the influence of ethnic traditional pottery and textiles with an individual contemporary interpretation.

Jane Perryman

Susan and Jim Whalen
(United States)

Vessel, w. 30 cm (11 ¾ in.), 2000.

Surface: Wax-resisted raku- and pit-fired stoneware. Low-fired, reduction.

This vessel was thrown from a regional yellow stoneware body, burnished and coated with terra sigillata. After bisquing to 890°C (1634°F), wax was applied using a sponge template to create patterns, thus organising the random chaotic markings of the pit firing. The vessel was fired in a raku kiln to 840°C (1544°F), and placed red-hot into oak sawdust for a further pit firing. Surface effects are created by salt and soda vaporisation during the raku stage, enriched by the random black markings of the pit firing.

Photograph: Tim Barnwell

For the past seven years we have been focusing on and working with the pit-firing process. We have gained more input into the results, but it is the raw, uncontrollable nature of the fire itself that keeps us fascinated, propelling the work in new directions. The rounded forms, ancient and universal, provide a canvas. Through exploration and refinement of these forms, we are searching into their mystery and meaning.

Susan and Jim Whalen

Duncan Ross (United Kingdom)

Terra Sigillata Bowl, h. 21 cm (8 ¼ in.), 2000.

Surface: Smoke-fired terra sigillata with resists and inlay. Low-fired earthenware, reduction.

This bowl was wheel-thrown of low-fired earthenware, and covered with varying densities of fine terra sigillata and resists, to promote varied smoke-fired colour effects. Fine clay inlay lines created controlled linear patterns and, after burnishing, the piece was placed in sawdust in saggars and fired several times at various temperatures.

Photograph: Duncan Ross

I use only clay and smoke – everything comes from that. Colours are achieved by smoke firing, and the decoration is developed from many sources including textiles and geometric motifs. I began working with terra sigillata from a desire to use the simplest materials with low-firing temperatures and to develop a rich surface with a combination of form and pattern that would be integral to the clay and allow the smoke process to play its essential and unpredictable part. From highly-complicated patterns using lines to create rhythms around the form, this extra dimension has released my linear pattern from its structure, allowing me to 'float' shapes onto the surface. I am always searching for development that comes from repetition; allowing the idea to flow from one group of work to the next, adding and omitting, to arrive at the ideal and most natural relationship of surface to form.

Duncan Ross

Jeff Shapiro (United States)

Extruder Form, h. 43 cm (17 in.), 2000.

Surface: Dripping ash glaze, wood-fired stoneware. High-fired, reduction.

This shape was made of a mixture of stoneware, porcelain and natural deposit clays extruded through a hydraulic compressor and loosely altered while still wet. Iron slip was applied to the dried piece, and it was once-fired in an Anagama kiln fuelled with ash wood, and lying on its side on seashell supports. Over an eight-day firing cycle to about 1300°C (2372°F), ash deposits dripped on the form from accumulations on silicon carbide shelves above.

Photograph: Bob Barrett

I chose the path of wood firing because I was attracted to the texture, the colour, and the 'imperfections' of nature reflected in the fired pieces of Bizen and Shigaraki ware that I first saw in museums and gallery shows. I also felt a strong desire to be connected to the process. Although my wood fire study in Japan took place in Bizen, I am not trying to produce Bizen ware. Personally, I am moving more towards a sculptural or architectural approach to creating new work, incorporating the archaic quality of wood firing and yet, bringing it into a contemporary context. Living in the middle of the woods has a subconscious effect on how I work. Sometimes, it may take years for that influence to actually surface in the work.

Jeff Shapiro

Rob Barnard (United States)

Covered Jar, h. 32 cm (12 ⅝ in.), 1998.

Surface: Ash-covered wood-fired stoneware. High-fired, reduction.

This wheel-thrown stoneware lidded jar was fired without applied slips or glazes in a wood-fired Anagama kiln for approximately 60 hours, to a temperature of about 1300°C (2372°F). Surface effects were entirely due to the movement of flames and ash throughout the kiln, with thicker ash fusing and melting on-surface at around 1230°C (2246°F), and sheltered surfaces providing varied contrasts to the thicker, runny ash deposits.

Photograph: Hubert Gentry

I have been making this type of wood-fired work for just over 30 years. I started in Japan in 1974. I had seen historical Japanese pieces in books, but had not been able to achieve the colours and the natural ash glaze that runs off the shoulder of pieces and down the belly. Form was my overriding concern and I had not until then found a way to 'finish' my forms. The abstract quality of the natural ash glaze and the flashing that occurs in this type of firing may not seem like 'surface decoration' but it is. It is more like the abstract quality of Mark Rothko's paintings, with two squares of colour, one placed above the other, than it is like the Impressionist and Post-Impressionist work that preceded it and the Pop Art that followed. It is a type of expression, a genre that has its own vocabulary. It is the language that I use.

Rob Barnard

Hozan Tanii (Japan)

Night Sky, 61.5 x 30.5 cm (24 ¼ x 12 in.), 2000.

Surface: Anagama-fired shell marks and straw fire-cord decoration. High-fired stoneware, reduction.

This platter for serving Japanese hors d'oeuvres was made from Shigaraki stoneware. Five pieces of twisted clay were rolled flat and a foot was applied with wirecut teeth. The piece was Anagama-fired to 1300°C (2372°F), for 4 ½ days, using red pine and other fuel woods. Surface markings occur through flashing and controlled effects (i.e. red marks from scallop shells, white circles from fire clay pads, fine lines from straw, and specks from erupting feldspar granules).

Photograph: Kensei Sugimoto

All ceramic materials are gifts from nature, a reflection of the mysterious depth and beauty of the patterns of change in our world. My wish is to combine nature's gifts with human thought and expression, to use the special tools of clay, glaze and firing to create objects that reveal our human sensibilities, translated from these gifts.

Hozan Tanii
Translated by Dorothy Feibleman

Yasuhiro Kohara
(Japan)

Flower Vase, h. 12 cm (4 ¾ in.), 1998.

Surface: *Bidoro* red pine ash dripping. High-fired stoneware, reduction.

This coil thrown vase was made with coarse Shigaraki stoneware, once-fired on its side in an Anagama kiln. Colour and pattern occur through the *bidoro* flow (natural ash deposit) and flame flashing marks. The piece was wood fired in reduction to about 1300°C (2372°F) with red pine.

Photograph: Kensei Sugimoto
Courtesy of Gallery Dai Ichi Arts Ltd, New York

I think of the 'bidoro' flow in the 'Anagama' firing as having the flowing characteristics of water as I load the kiln. The variations of the flow, the jewel-like green of the natural ash, are dependent on the vagaries of firing, and as such reflect the mutability of water itself in a natural landscape.

Yasuhiro Kohara

Don Reitz (United States) OPPOSITE

Punch Out, h. 20.5 cm (8 in.), w. 12.5 cm (5 in.), 2000.

Surface: Kaolin and dripped ash on stoneware. High-fired, reduction.

This piece was handbuilt by literally punching out a halved block of clay with a thick, square piece of wood. After loosely wirecutting the surface, and adding a clay strip, the piece was sprayed overall with a thin coating of Avery kaolin, and subsequently wood fired with oak over four days in an Anagama kiln. Drip marks occur from ash deposits from kiln shelves above.

Photograph: Jeff Bruce

Over the years my clay objects have evolved into a three-dimensional canvas which I can push, pull, strike, and draw into. The fire adds its own painterly qualities to the surface. Although it is orchestrated by the artist, the flame eventually brings forth its unique palette. As an object nears its completion I am most excited. It has already led to the next project, or has redefined a concept that I am working on at the present. Each object that is created, in a way, defeats previous objects and stands on its own. The past is relevant to the future, but my work is not about the past. The best is yet to come.

Don Reitz

Janet Mansfield
(Australia)

Jar, h. 49 cm (19 ¼ in.), 1999.

Surface: Eucalyptus ash, Anagama-fired. High-fired stoneware, reduction.

The large jar was wheel-thrown in three sections, joined when leatherhard, made from local clay blended with sand and feldspar to withstand prolonged firing. Loosely-incised clay sgraffito lines serve to catch ash deposits in the kiln. The jar was fired for three days in an Anagama kiln to 1350°C (2462°F) using local eucalyptus wood as fuel. The yellow wood ash contrasts strongly with the deep red clay colour.

Photograph: Ian Hobbs

I like making these large jars, not only for the opportunity to decorate them with patterns of leaves and grasses I see outside the workshop window, but for the challenge they give, being able to withstand extreme temperatures over such a long time. I enjoy all the processes of making pots from the mixing of the clay, to the research techniques, and to the aesthetic considerations of form and use and beauty. The colours from the rocks and earth around me, the soft forms of my landscape, the calm of the country environment, all play a part in inspiring me. Life and work should be interrelated.

Janet Mansfield

Claude Champy
(France)

Double-Walled Vase, h. 56 cm (22 in.), w. 29 cm (11 ¼ in.), 2000.

Surface: Wood-fired, saturated oxide glazes. High-fired stoneware, reduction.

This vase, loosely slab constructed of grogged stoneware to withstand firing stresses, is double-walled and was bisqued in a gas kiln to 900°C (1652°F). A chrome oxide-saturated black feldspathic glaze, and a white titanium/zinc glaze were freely dipped and poured, and the piece was wood fired in reduction to 1300°C (2372°F) over 15–20 hours.

Photograph: Jean-Jacques Morer

Cracks, deformations, crawling, flaws, under- and over-glazing – all these so-called faults can be used expressively. In complicity with my clay and glazes, comfortably seated in front of my wood kiln, surrounded by piles of wood and convivial friends, I put my faith in the fire. My personal 'Internet' is a pile of bricks in the shape of a kiln – all that I require!

Claude Champy

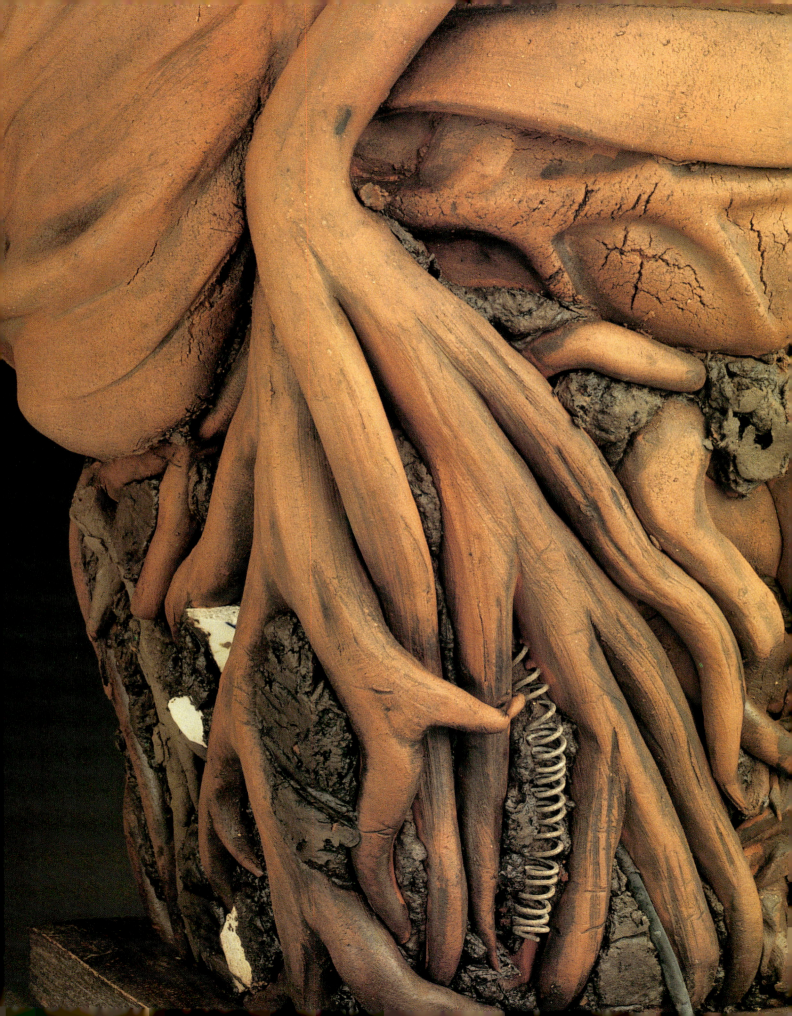

chapter ten

Unconventional approaches

By unconventional approaches I mean the use of materials and techniques not traditionally associated with ceramic procedures. Questions about what is 'proper' and 'conventional', acceptable practice, what is radical innovation, to the point of being 'anti-ceramic' – these are all entirely subjective as far as I am concerned. To my mind the integrity of the maker's intention should be apparent in the strength and maturity of the final work and its particular role. Certainly I would not drink from a vessel designed for drinking but coated inside with urethane. As an outside surface treatment in a non-utilitarian context – why not? Some of the unconventional approaches presented here include: use of organic materials, use of found objects, use of non-ceramic materials (and the list is surprisingly innovative and extensive; i.e. acrylics, urethane, detergent, wax), sandblasting and eroded surfaces, acid-etching, faux-shards and gold-leaf – *vive la diversité*!

Linda Huey (United States)

Root Bound, h. 58.5 cm (23 in.), w. 33 cm (13 in.), 1998.

Surface: Clay and miscellaneous debris bonded with hay clay. Low-fired earthenware, oxidation.

This piece was handbuilt inside a cardboard form, with root shapes made from terracotta earthenware, and interspersed with various bits of debris (shards, metal springs, nails, etc.). These were all backed and bonded with hay clay, a clay/hay/glaze/grog/manganese mixture that does not crack in firing. After bisquing, a low-fired glaze was applied to the inside and top, stain to the outside, and the piece was fired in oxidation to 1050°C (1922°F).

Photograph: Linda Huey

I live in an isolated part of western New York State where the abundance of the natural environment inspires my work. I am surrounded by many sources of natural ideas and influences. Forces of nature, such as growth, intrigue me. In 'Root Bound' large, full leaves spring from small, compressed roots and dirt that contain mosaic-like bits of trash. This becomes a subtle environmental statement about our threat to the survival of nature.

Linda Huey

Jenny Beavan (United Kingdom)

Plate Movement, 45 x 53 x 22 cm (17 ¾ x 21 x 8 ⅝ in.), 1996.

Surface: Direct rock-impressed slab shape with fused indigenous materials. High-fired T-material, oxidation.

This form was constructed from slab impressions taken directly from rocks on site. The clay was of a T-material type. Beach sands, minerals and river mud were layered with texture, with coloured slips and glazes for contrast. Fusion of these diverse materials took place in an electric firing at 1240°C (2264°F).

Photograph: Takashi Hatakeyama

My work has become an interrelated series of processes, involving my perception of a place, in combination with sympathetic forms to convey a sense of spirit of that place. I gather beach sands, minerals from disused mine workings, river muds rich in spoils from the mines, and secondary constituents found in clay lakes and spoil tips. I use these waste materials to build up texture and surface contrast on my vessel forms and, in the process, subject the materials to yet another series of changes. The links which I perceive between the development of the vessel in ceramics, and the development of the geological vessel of the Earth, lead me on a journey in the exploration of changed states of matter: decay, disintegration, movement, re-location and re-formation. My aim in the finished piece is to suggest a moment in a process of change.

Jenny Beavan

Richard Burkett (United States)

Pressure Vessel Series No. 3, h. 20 cm (8 in.), w. 15 cm (6 in.), 2000.

Surface: Soda-fired porcellaneous stoneware with blown-out organic materials and metal components. High-fired, oxidation.

This vessel form was made of wheel-thrown porcellaneous stoneware with an inner container form, and an outer form containing organic burn-out materials (toasted buckwheat groats, wheat, soybeans, etc.) mixed into the clay. A very slow prolonged bisque allows the organics to slowly outgas without explosively destroying the form. A fake Avery kaolin flashing slip was eroded by the subsequent soda firing to 1300°C (2372°F), and metal components were added.

Photograph: Richard Burkett

Occasional aspects of my work are drawn from memories of dealing with the oddly functional farm implements and tools left to me by my grandfather. Other elements may come from memories of chemical glassware in my father's laboratory. Added to that is an ongoing concern for family history and more generally, for domestic issues, shared space, and responsibilities. It's all a reaction to living in a heavily industrialised, fast-paced world, which forces one to balance the mechanical with the personal, the impersonal with the poetical. An ongoing series celebrates both the industrial worker and the ability to make do with what is at hand. The work often incorporates found industrial salvage objects which are used as handles or lids.

Richard Burkett

Claudi Casanovas (Spain)

L'Afrau, 120 x 74 cm (47 ¼ x 28 ⅜ in.), 1996.

Surface: Clay blended with non-ceramic materials, chiselled and sandblasted. High-fired stoneware, reduction.

This massive container form was made using stoneware clay from La Borne in France, blended with a mixture of other materials such as wood shavings, feldspathic and volcanic rock fragments, styrofoam chips, straw and low-fired clays. Layers of this clay mix were slab constructed inside a plaster mould form and, once dry, the surface was altered with a hammer and chisel. After gas firing in reduction to 1300°C (2372°F), a final surface sandblasting took place.

Photograph: F. Goalec

The group of fossil forms Pedra Foguera *(flint) emerged from a desire to combine the idea of the traditional, open, food-containing vessel with a knowledge of the Earth's basic material structure, and a curiosity about remote origins and lost traditions. The container can reflect a number of things — human containment and possibility of fulfilment, emptiness and silence, death and rebirth…*

Claudi Casanovas

Jim Leedy (United States)

Ribbon Plate, d. 66 cm (26 in.), 1998.

Surface: Thrown, folded and manipulated clay with bronze, iron and glass additions. High-fired stoneware, salt glazed, reduction.

This organically-occurring plate was wheel-thrown, trimmed, refolded, pushed and compressed, after layering with porcelain slip. Further stretching, distorting and slip re-application took place – much like an action painting – and bronze, iron and glass chunks were pressed into the wet surface. Once dry, the plate was once-fired in a salt kiln to 1315°C (2399°F).

Photograph: Jim Walker

I attempt to ignore everything I have learned when I am creating. I try to become one with nature, to flow freely as a tree grows or a stream flows, directed only by the forces of resistance that nature has established. Of course, learned information can never be completely erased from any activity, since I am the result of everything that I have learned until this moment. But, by consciously using collective information I attempt to work intuitively. I hope to create work that is not contrived, while revealing process and using all elements of creation, from the mark of my hands and tools, to the evidence of flame striking the work during firing.

Jim Leedy

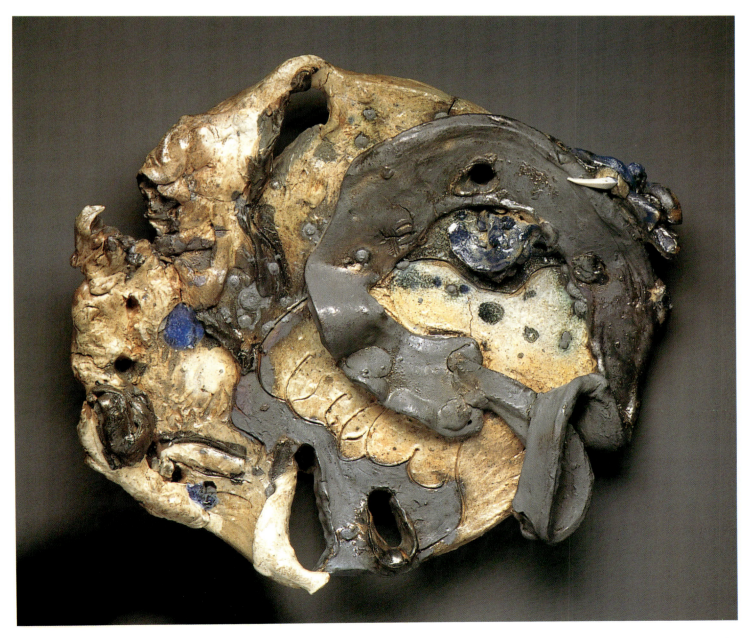

Robin Welch (United Kingdom)

Red Over Blue, 26 x 36 cm (10 ¼ x 14 ⅛ in.), 2000.

Surface: Slips, dry-clay crumbs, underglaze colours, oxides and enamels. Multiple firings, stoneware, reduction.

This double-sided stoneware slab structure was conceived as a complex abstract 'painting', building up layers upon layers of texture and colour. These included porcelain slip, with adhering fire-clay crumbs, presenting a textured white 'canvas'. While still damp, underglaze colours with black and white slips were applied and, after drying and bisquing, a coating of matt white glaze, reduction fired to 1200–1300°C (2192°–2372°F), became the background for further coloured earthenware glazes, and several more firings down the temperature scale.

Photograph: Graham Murrel
Courtesy of Lynne Strover Gallery

My images, textures and colours are based loosely, but not entirely, on the Australian outback landscape. Further inspiration has come to me from such diverse painters as Arthur Boyd, Fred Williams, Mark Rothko and Robert Ryman. In this work, I attempt to bring my painting and ceramics closer together.

Robin Welch

Neil Tetkowski (United States) OPPOSITE

Open Mandala, 88 x 101 cm (34 ⅝ x 39 ¾ in.), 1998.

Surface: Clay, iron and steel embedded in earthenware. Mid-firing range, reduction.

This large shape was thrown from 150 lb (68 kg) of red earthenware clay, radically altered when wet, and incised with a saw blade and railway spike. Iron and steel bolts and spikes were embedded in the clay and when dry, the piece was sprayed with thin terra sigillata and a high-frit clear glaze. The piece was once fired with salt in a gas kiln, with a short reduction, to 1150°C (2102°F). Large spots on surface occurred due to interaction of rock-salt chunks on the terra sigillata.

Photograph: Eva Heyd

Large or small, everybody makes a mark on the Earth. As an artist I make my mark on the clay. The artwork always makes a reference to the Earth and the environment we live in and constantly alter. Often I mix other materials with clay and like to fire them together. Handprints or carved lines suggest a passage of time and an interaction of different energies. I like stretching and pulling this material that so easily expresses movement and flow of energy. Natural forces of the wind, water currents and erosion interest me. Human energy and nature's energy represent a kind of yin and yang. There is balance, there is conflict, but ultimately it is all just one energy. Nature always takes back.

Neil Tetkowski

John Chalke (Canada)

Thin Cup and Red Sky, h. 17 cm (16 ¾ in.), w. 30 cm (11 ¾ in.), 2000.
Surface: Found shards embedded in stoneware slab. Low-fired, oxidation.

This wall piece was rolled out as a stoneware slab and altered with two found shards (outer white, inner blue willow pattern) forming a cup shape, and bonded with slip. After bisquing, the shards were further bonded with glaze, and the upper red and black section was glazed with a lead/chrome glaze. The lower half was glazed with a silicon/carbide mixture, with added blue lumps of mostly sand, mixed with flour, frit and copper, and rolled as spheres. The piece was electric fired in oxidation to 1070°C (1958°F).

Photograph: Barbara Tipton

As well as sometimes making a reference back to a historical ceramic period through conventional means, such as shape, glaze or handle, I refer back with shards, sprig moulds or other identities from earlier periods on top of works from this moment – if one of course can ever isolate these things. So there seems to be a lot of hybridisation – not really much different now that I think of it, from many works I see around me by others. It all happens in the studio, that put-aside sacred area, one of forgiveness much of the time, where faults and mistakes may survive before others' silent, harmless jeering. Once inside, anything may happen. It's our church and sanctuary, and our confessional base.

John Chalke

Dan Anderson (United States) OPPOSITE

One Gallon Gas Can, h. 30 cm (11 ¾ in.), w. 20.5 cm (8 in.), 1999.
Surface: Soda-fired layered slips and glazes with decals, sandblasting and wire. High-fired stoneware, reduction.

This 'gas can' shape was made of a stoneware and rough brick earthenware mix, full of impurities. Thrown and dented after bisquing, alternating layers of Shino glaze, slip, copper stoneware glaze and more slip were applied, to the point of flaking off. The piece was soda fired, with soda ash, baking soda and lithium sprayed directly into the kiln (around 1215°C/2219°F) and fired up to 1300°C (2372°F). After firing, a low-fired decal was applied, further sandblasting took place, and household wire was attached to nichrome wire embedded and fired into the clay.

Photograph: Jeffery M. Bruce
Courtesy of Gail Severn Gallery, Idaho

My ceramics, an amalgam of vessel and industrial artefact, are full of irony – handmade replicas of man-made objects, soft clay renderings of hard metal objects, aged and impotent reminders of a once-powerful age. The usefulness of machines in their original states is limited – as the products of progress, they're doomed to obsolescence – but by recreating them in a 'primitive' medium, I believe they will endure through the ages. They have been transformed for eternity into art. In this way, too, I have taken the aesthetic and political ugliness out of industry, reminding everyone that change can be both hurtful/traumatic and positive/healing, once again underscoring the power of art to uplift the human condition.

Dan Anderson

Léopold Foulem (Canada)

So Many Men, So Little Time, h. 36.5 cm (14 ⅜ in.), w. 25 cm (9 ⅞ in.), 1993-1997.

Surface: Found metal parts and earthenware with decals and lustres. Low-fired, oxidation.

This vessel shape was made of a rolled-out earthenware slab, cut from a paper template a little larger than required, to allow for shrinkage. Several cylinder shapes were made and wheel-trimmed, from which one was selected to fit the found metal base and lid components. Once bisqued, the piece was glazed with transparent glaze, electric fired to 990°C (1814°F), covered with applied cut-out decals and some lustre, and refired to 700°C (1292°F). The metal and ceramic components were then fitted together.

Photograph: Raymonde Bergeron

Courtesy of Prime Gallery, Toronto

For a number of years I have been using the concept of 'mounted porcelain' as a framework for various series of works. Whereas the European 'marchands merciers' were making elaborate bronze mounts for the rare and precious oriental porcelain brought to them by their clients, my strategy is totally different. The 'found objects' are the metal parts gathered at flea markets, garage sales and antique shops; the ceramic inserts are made to fit the settings. In So Many Men, So Little Time, the structure of the two dimensional composition, in which Santa Claus is located off centre, is reminiscent of Chinese porcelain prototypes where written text is presented. As in many Chinese artifacts, there is a sexual content intended in the iconography. Here Santa Claus stands for the 'dirty old men' of the world and the purple grapes crowning the cylindrical vessel are to be read as 'fruits', a euphemism for gay men.

Léopold Foulem

Gotlind Weigel (Germany)

Large Teapot, h. 15 cm (5 ⅞ in.), w. 20 cm (7 ⅞ in.), 1997.

Surface: Tape-resisted, limestone-glazed stoneware with wooden base construction. High-fired, reduction.

The teapot shape was thrown with Westerwald stoneware, cut and reassembled. After bisquing, unglazed areas were masked off with tape and a limestone glaze was sprayed on. The lid was glazed in a dark iron ash blue glaze, and the piece was gas fired in reduction to 1350°C (2462°F). Iron spotting from the clay was encouraged. Integral to the piece is the wooden base, made of black-stained beech.

Photograph: Werner Baumann

My work is directly inspired by nature: stones, shells, the curves of windswept desert sand dunes. Initially, I was strongly influenced by the aesthetics of the Bauhaus, and found myself drawn to the painters Van Gogh, Manet, Cézanne, and the early works of Picasso. Later the words of Feininger and Morandi touched my sensibilities, and today the works of architects Frank Gehry and Zaha Hadid, as well as those of packaging genius Christo still inspire me. The teapot has been a theme to which I have returned again and again over the last 50 years. Manifold shapes can still flower within the framework of function.

Gotlind Weigel

Paolo Staccioli (Italy)

Cavalli (Horses), h. 33 cm (13 in.), 2000.

Surface: Wire-wrapped earthenware with metallic oxides, sulphates and nitrates. Low-fired, alternating reduction and oxidation.

This vase shape was slipcast and thrown, using a red earthenware clay, and covered entirely with an opaque white slip. After bisquing to 950°C (1742°F), the outline drawing was made with an underglaze pencil, and background colours were painted in using metallic oxides, sulphates and nitrates. A transparent glaze was sprayed over, the neck was wrapped in copper wire, and the piece was gas fired to 930°C (1706°F), with alternating reduction and oxidation phases.

Photograph: Andrea Dughetti

I am basically self-taught, and started to draw early on in life, mostly landscapes and still life. The idea of the contour line has always captivated me, and the work of the painter Paolo Uccello (AD 1396–1475), with his dynamic representations of horses, has formed the basis of a visual morphology of horse imagery, present in both my ceramic and sculptural work.

Paolo Staccioli

Bennett Bean (United States)

Triple On Base, h. 45.5 cm (17 ⅞ in.), w. 78.5 cm (31 in.), 1998.

Surface: Pit-fired earthenware with gilt, acrylics and urethane. Low-fired, reduction.

This piece was constructed of thrown, trimmed, cut and reassembled white earthenware, which was sanded when dry and painted with white terra sigillata. After polishing, the piece was bisqued and decorative motifs were applied using black pressure-sensitive graphic tapes and an adhesive mask. Selected areas were waxed, others glazed, both wax and tape acting as a glaze resist. The piece was wood fired in an open pit to blow off tape and melt glazed areas, as well as to create flashing effects on unglazed areas. Upon cooling, the interior was prepared with several coats of gesso-spackle, sanded between coats, with three subsequent coats of red clay, and finally water-polished. This surface was then sealed, sized and gilded. Exterior areas where tape and mask had burned off were painted with acrylic, and the vessel was sealed with urethane gel.

Photograph: Bennett Bean

The idea of control, in my case, takes the form of refusing to let the fire have the last word. So much of the embellishment of these pieces is done after the firing, i.e. the paint and the gold. These pieces are accumulated evidence of my behaviour, each step leaving a mark. At 57 I'm familiar with both myself and the elements that I am working with. This allows considerable freedom and relaxation.

Bennett Bean

Jim Thomson (Canada)

February Boboli, h. 51 cm (20 in.), w. 35 cm (13 ¾ in.), 1997.

Surface: Clay crumb surface and dishwasher detergent over iron slip. High-fired stoneware, oxidation.

This piece was fired at cone 6 (1200°C/2192°F) and was made from thrown and altered stoneware clay. The grid lid is a cut-out slab. The vessel's textured white area was achieved by slipping clay crumbs onto the leatherhard surface. Once bisqued, white slip was applied and then dabbed over with a high-magnesium crusty crawl glaze. The dark glaze was achieved by mixing one part local clay with one part wood ash. The mixture was passed through a kitchen sieve and then ballmilled for 30 minutes. The brown surface of the stand is dishwasher detergent fired over iron slip.

Photograph: Jim Thomson
Courtesy of Prime Gallery, Toronto

Often I am intrigued by what a functional object is doing when it is not being used. The grimy surface of my used wok hanging in the kitchen has a patina that tells a story. I associate the surface with cuisine, smell, taste, recipes, family, conversation, personal history and so on. I use surface as part of the means to express the exploration of the relationship of what an object is to what an object does.

Jim Thomson

Antje Scharfe (Germany)

Still-Leben Gefässe (Still Life Vessels), 80 x 60 cm (31 ⅝ x 23 ½ in.), 1996.

Surface: Direct-wet-poured bone china on kiln shelves. High-fired porcelain, oxidation.

These flat 'vessels' were created by direct pouring of a high bone ash-content porcelain slip onto kiln shelves covered with kiln wash. Fine slip details were added immediately by brushing and trailing for an overall loose-edged organic visual effect, and some stain drawing was added for details. The pieces were once fired flat (as poured) to 1220°C (2228°F) in oxidation, with very slow cooling because of extreme lateral shrinkage. The flat 'vessels' are mounted upright, embedded in a paraffin/clay base.

Photograph: Gandlitz & Gloede

Every ceramicist is usually asked 'What is your relationship with the vessel?' In this case, my purpose is to transcend the vessel's function in the conventional 'container' sense, free it from volume and hand use to serve the heart and brain, as a still life, a painting, or a thought-provoking visual image.

Antje Scharfe

Michael Sherrill (United States)

Lovers' Leaves, h. 25.5 cm (10 in.), w. 91.5 cm (36 in.), 2000.
Surface: Multi-layered abraded and polished porcelain slips and glazes. High-fired, oxidation.

The leaf shapes were made from extruded, pulled tubes of porcelain clay, triangulated, with added modelled rib surfaces. The shapes were sealed off, and air was sucked out with a vacuum pump, to give the shapes a natural curl. Several layers of coloured calcined slips were applied, with successive bisque firings and abrasion of slips in between. Finally a hard transparent glaze was applied, fired to 1220°C (2228°F) in oxidation, and further hand abraded and polished for a skin-like surface.

Photograph: Michael Sherrill

I consider myself one raised under the influence of the Moderns. My work before this series was a study in simplicity and refinement in search of the spiritual. But something happened. I moved into a new studio that allowed the natural world to be right in front of me. As a result, it became important to express the impact of this renewed sense of wonder. I believe that somehow the things that impact upon me internally, and stimulate me visually, are great indicators of my own aesthetic. In nature, you might pick up a leaf and marvel at its beauty and colour. If you set that leaf aside, and then come back to it later, it will no longer look like the same leaf. The moment has passed. I'm reaching to find that same sense of the transcendent moment, and to share it with the viewer.

Michael Sherrill

Steve Fullmer (New Zealand)

Rose Can, h. 240 cm (94 ½ in.), w. 120 cm (47 ¾ in.), 2000.

Surface: Water-eroded layered slips and glaze. Low-fired earthenware, oxidation.

This large vessel was wheel-thrown, using red earthenware, with slight shape distortion. After bisquing to 1000°C (1832°F), the piece was hosed down with water, followed by a sprayed coating of iron sulphate and coloured slip. This process was repeated several times, with final brush and sponge on-surface highlighting, followed by an overall spray of white slip, which was then hosed off in areas to reveal various layers. A final coat of clear glaze was applied, then almost completely brushed off, to be absorbed into the slip and enhance colour. The final firing was to 1160°C (2120°F) in oxidation.

Photograph: Steve Fullmer

Born in Portland, Oregon in 1946, raised in Los Angeles from the age of five, ate hamburgers, surfed and worked on my cars until I was drafted into the US Army 1966–1968. Enrolled into a pottery class in 1970, made Dobro guitars for the Dopera brothers who invented the National Steel guitars. Between the pottery and the guitars I learned to be a craftsman. Emigrated to New Zealand in 1973 and established my own workshop in Nelson in 1976. Married, three children, dog, cat, mortgage. New Zealand has a lot of erosion, wind, rain, sunshine, waves pounding beaches. My technique has possibly evolved from living life in New Zealand.

Steve Fullmer

Michael Cleff (Germany)

Untitled, h. 32 cm (12 ⅝ in.) 1998.

Surface: Post-firing hand-ground Shino-glazed stoneware. High-fired, reduction.

The shape was handbuilt using an iron content stoneware, from an initial self-made one-piece plaster mould. Once the hollow form in clay was established, holes were cut in and, after prolonged careful drying, the piece was bisqued. A Shino glaze was applied by brush in several layers, and the piece was gas fired in strong reduction to 1300°C (2372°F). Afterwards a silicon carbide rough grinder was used over the surface, followed by wet hand-grinding using fine diamond-faced grinding blocks. Various subtle stone-like surfaces can be achieved this way.

Photograph: Christian Schlüter

My interest in architecture and minimal art has led to the creation of basic archetypal shapes that need not necessarily be mathematically exact. Deliberate light asymmetry and irregular treatment of edges provide a certain intrinsic dynamism to an otherwise static form. Cut-out elements create an important relationship between inner volume and outer shape, and my system of 'controlled haphazardness', inherent in the making process, maintains a slightly ambivalent aesthetic; controlled shape allied to organic surface. The stone-like character of the ground-down glaze surface provides a subtle palette of colour and texture, attracting both eye and hand.

Michael Cleff

Greg Daly (Australia)

Bowl, d. 65 cm (25 ½ in.), 1990.

Surface: Acid-etched lustre with enamel decoration. Low-fired stoneware, oxidation.

This shallow thrown bowl, made of porcellaneous stoneware, was glazed with a high-feldspar cobalt glaze, and gas fired in oxidation to 1300°C (2372°F). Gold/bismuth lustres and enamels were applied, and the bowl was refired to 730°C (1346°F). Patterns were resisted using hot wax and tape, and the surface was painted with hydrofluoric acid. The acid and resists were removed with water and detergent to prevent scumming and to neutralise the acid.

Photograph: R. Baader

An acid-etched surface provides a foil for a lustre or high-gloss surface. The acid etches through the masking lustre, to reveal glaze colours and a smooth, satin matt surface below, unlike a sandblasted surface, which can remain rough to the touch.

Greg Daly

Richard Milette (Canada)

Three-Legged Teapot, h. 17.5 cm (6 ⅞ in.), w. 27 cm (10 ⅝ in.), 1994.

Surface: Faux-shard surface over thrown form, with decals, enamels and metallic lustre. Low-fired earthenware, oxidation.

This teapot consists of an inner shell thrown of white earthenware, with a faux-shard outer shell, composed of deliberately broken pieces. The shards float above the inner shell and show visible gaps. Press moulded additions form feet, spout and handle. After careful drying and bisquing, the shard surfaces were resisted with latex and the piece was glazed in its entirety. Latex was removed from the shards, which was handpainted using coloured glazes, and glaze-fired in oxidation to 1000°C (1832°F). Finally, decals – black enamel and gold lustre – were applied and fired to 780°C (1436°F). Enamels and lustres were repainted and a fourth and final firing occurred, again at 780°C (1436°F).

Photograph: Raymonde Bergeron
Courtesy of Prime Gallery, Toronto

The shape of the teapot presented here is stereotypical: I borrowed it, I did not invent it. The shards, which appear to be floating in the air, reconstruct the contour of the body of the teapot. The other parts are attachments to the body so that the resulting object is indisputably recognisable as a teapot. The core of the teapot body, to which the shards are structurally joined, has been glazed black so as to negate its materiality and posit it as space. All the shards are fabricated rather than actual. They are imitations rather than reproductions. The restrained diversity of the pseudo-historical shards is meant to emphasise the importance of the concept over that of the narrative. The intentional use of different faux-materials questions the significance and traditional hierarchy of materials within a cultural context. The resulting work is about the teapot as subject and as object.

Richard Milette

Roswitha Wulff (Australia) OPPOSITE

Vessel Form, h. 12 cm (4 ¾ in.), 1997.

Surface: Gold leaf over imprinted shell marks. High-fired stoneware, reduction.

This stoneware shape was wheel-thrown and altered to square with a paddle. It was covered in a Shino-type clay/feldspar slip and wood fired to 1300°C (2372°F), supported on its side on three seashells. After firing these were subsequently coated with gold leaf.

Photograph: Jan Thijs

I am attracted to the wood-fired pot by the total carelessness of how each mark is made, as if delivered by chance. The appeal of the object lives in this apparent indifference to the maker. The results, achieved through deliberate skill, effort and nurturing are visible, but should not be seen as the outcome of explicit action. For form, my influence comes from Art Nouveau, techniques are informed by pottery from Japan, and my colours are inspired by the Australian landscape. Using the language of wood firing, I create a personal vocabulary with new subjects, grammar and syntax, that make of each pot a one-off object, containing all.

Roswitha Wulff

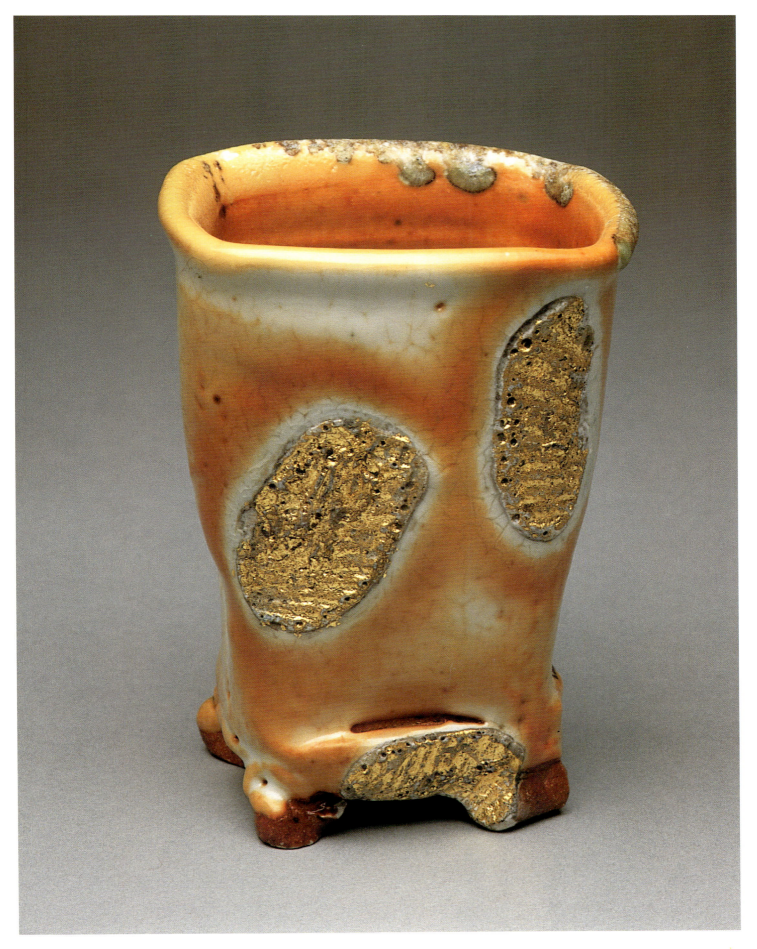

Glossary of terms and techniques

Airbrushing: The practice of applying surface colour through a compressed-air spray nozzle.

Anagama (kiln): A Japanese-style wood-fired cross-draught kiln, usually on a slope, with chimney at top and fire box at bottom; promotes flame markings and ash deposits on wares.

Bisque: The first firing, usually to a lower temperature, to create a bonded and porous clay body suitable for wet-glazing.

Bone china: A porcelain-like clay using bone ash as a body flux, with limited plasticity, and a high-bisque and low-glaze temperature; more suitable for slipcasting.

Bourry-box kiln: One in which a separate combustion chamber attached to the main ware chamber promotes a cleaner firing and alleviates flying ash deposits in the kiln.

Celadon: A feldspathic high-fire semi-translucent glaze, usually in green tones, taking its colour from red iron oxide changed in a reducing fire.

China paints: See overglaze enamels.

Clay inlay (*mishima*): From the Korean; a technique of incising or stamping pattern into clay, filling it with thick contrasting slip, and scraping it flush for an inlaid pattern.

Coperta (crystallina): A thin, usually sprayed coating of transparent glaze over in-glaze brushwork, sometimes used over maiolica.

Crackle (glaze): one in which crazing or fine crack surface lines are encouraged as a pattern attribute, sometimes emphasised through rubbed-in dyes.

Crystalline glaze: A glaze containing crystals; promoted by controlled seeding and cooling during which essential oxides are separated from surrounding fluid glaze to form crystals.

Cuerda seca: Using wax dyed with oxides to separate fields of glaze; leaves a dark unglazed separating line.

Decal: See transfer.

Drapemoulding: The practice of shaping slabs of clay over a pre-shaped mould.

Earthenware: A low-firing clay body usually not fully vitrified.

Engobe: See slip.

Firing temperatures (approximate): Low-firing range: below 1100/1120°C (2012°/2948°F); mid-firing range: from 1100/1120°C (2012°/2948°F) to 1170/1200°C (2138°/2192°F); high-firing range: above 1200/1300°C (2192°/2372°F).

Flashing slip: A clay slip designed to respond in colour to flame marks and flashing in a fuel-fired kiln.

Frit: Part of a glaze recipe that has already been melted and reground for inclusion into a glaze, usually at lower temperatures.

Gas firing: Firing with natural gas, usually in a cross-draught kiln; for a softer flame, requiring a forced air burner.

Gesso-spackle: A fine grade non-vinyl plaster-like filler for preparing a gesso-like ground.

Glaze firing: The second firing (after the bisque) to fuse the glaze coating to the clay body, usually at a higher temperature.

Gold-leaf (gilding): Very finely pounded sheets of gold attached to oil-sized paper, cut out and removed and carefully glued (without firing) to the fired ceramic surface.

Greenware: Unfired dry ceramic wares.

Grog (Molochite, chamotte): A refractory ground body (i.e. white Molochite) added to clays for tensile strength, shrinkage reduction, and extra tooth and texture.

Hakeme: From the Korean; the use of coarse brushes and thick slip to promote a textural and gestural pattern.

Handbuilding: The practice of clay construction without the use of the wheel (i.e. slab building, pinching, coiling, etc.).

In-glaze (painting): The practice of painting with stains and oxides onto a raw-glaze surface; pattern fuses into the glaze during glaze firing.

Laminating: The practice of bonding together contrasting layers of clays (liquid or leatherhard).

Latex emulsion: A water-based resist material that when dry can be peeled away to allow for further patterning on the resisted area.

Leatherhard: The state of clay in which it is no longer malleable, but retains enough moisture for bonding of components (i.e. spouts, handles, knobs, etc.).

Lustres: Metallic surfaces, such as gold, silver, platinum, copper, bronze, etc., created by metal compounds reducing to pure metal on-surface in a third low-firing (around 750°C/1382°F), after application to an already glaze-fired surface. Lustres in oxidation tend to be flat and uniform; in reduction, halos and colour variations can occur.

Macrocrystalline glaze: one in which very large surface crystals are visible.

Maiolica: Tin-glazed wares (historical or contemporary) or a tin- or zircon-opacified glaze, used for painting bright colours on a white ground in the low-firing range; (not to be confused with 'Majolica'; a range of ornate Victorian wares produced by the Minton factory in England in the mid-1800s).

***Mishima* inlay:** See clay inlay.

Molochite: See grog.

Neriage: From the Japanese (pronounced *neddi-ah-gay*); the practice of joining coloured clays together on the wheel, and throwing them for a marbleised effect.

Nerikomi (*millefiori*): The practice of layering or rolling together coloured clays, cutting them in cross-section patterns, and joining them together (usually pressed into moulds).

Nitrates: See soluble metal salts.

Oilspot (*Yuteki*): A high-fired dark glaze in

which impure iron particles erupt into the surface and crystallise into spots unable to be absorbed into the high-iron-content surrounding glaze; requires an oxidising firing.

On-glaze (painting): The practice of applying imagery (lustres, transfers, overglaze enamels) onto an already glaze-fired surface, and firing again at a much lower temperature.

Overglaze enamels (on-glaze enamels, china paints): Bright ceramic soft-firing glazes, usually in an oil-based medium, applied to an already glaze-fired surface and third-fired, usually to about 750°C (1382°F). Since they do not fully integrate with the glaze surface, they can wear down in time and are mostly used for exterior accent and highlight painting.

Oxidation: The atmosphere in a kiln where a surplus of oxygen is present (normal in electric kilns), forced air in fuel-fired kilns.

Oxides (metal): Materials forming the fluxes, opacifiers and, most commonly, the colours in a glaze: cobalt for blue, copper for green, iron for brown/black, etc., with many variations, depending on inter-mixture, glaze base, kiln atmosphere and firing temperature.

Paper clay: A compound of shredded paper pulp and clay with both green and dry strength, allowing for the formation of very thin sheets; fires like a normal body when paper has burned way.

Parian paste: A soft-paste porcellaneous material with a higher flux than clay content, usually used for unglazed work, firing up to 1200°C (2192°F).

Photo transfers: Photographic imagery that has been printed in oil-based ceramic inks, for application to an already glaze-fired surface (see transfer) for third-firing at low temperatures (usually around 750°C/1382°F).

Porcelain: A fine, white, homogeneous, high-vitrifying clay, that integrates with the glaze to the point of translucency, when thin-walled and very high-fired.

Pressmoulding: The practice of creating shapes by pressing clay into pre-shaped moulds.

Propane firing: Firing with bottled liquid petroleum gas, for a harder flame, not requiring a draught, but less easy to direct in the kiln.

Raku (firing): A rapid low-firing procedure where wares are placed in a hot kiln for firing, withdrawn while still hot, and placed in combustible material for rapid surface reduction while cooling, before the glaze has set.

Raw glazing: The practice of glazing unbisqued wares, usually to be once fired only.

Reduction: The atmosphere in a fuel-fired kiln where oxygen is deliberately curtailed in order to promote special glaze surface/colour effects.

Saggar: A protective clay container used in a fuel-fired kiln to protect wares from flying ash deposits.

Salt glaze: A high-fire glaze derived from salt being introduced into a kiln fire, where the salt volatilises, and sodium oxide, in the salt, combines with aluminium oxide and silica, in the clay, to form a glaze skin. Developed in the Rhineland in Germany in the late 14th century.

Serigraphic screenprinting: The process of creating a printed image by pressing inks through a patterned fine screen mesh.

Sgraffito: The practice of scratching through one layer of colour (clay, slip, glaze, stains, etc.) to reveal the layer below.

Slab construction: The practice of creating shapes by assembling rolled out flat slabs of clay.

Slip (engobe): Any liquid or semi-liquid clay, used for joining clay components, for slipcasting, or coloured for decoration purposes.

Slipcasting: The practice of pouring liquid clay (slip) into plaster moulds to create shapes, before partial drying and assembly.

Slumpmoulding: The practice of creating forms by pushing clay slabs into a hollow mould form.

Soaking: The practice of maintaining kiln temperature at an even level for a prolonged period, usually at the end of a firing cycle.

Soda firing: The introduction into a kiln fire of sodium (usually as sodium carbonate and bicarbonate) which bonds with the clay body to form a glaze skin (usually at high temperatures).

Soluble metal salts: Metals in water-soluble form (i.e. sulphates, nitrates, chlorides, acetates); used for colour penetration into a surface, and to promote even colour washes (without particle interference) at all temperatures, in conjunction with unglazed, glazed and lustre surfaces.

Sprig: A small three-dimensional clay shape extracted from a plaster or bisque stamp mould, and applied at the leatherhard stage as low-relief decoration.

Stoneware: A mid-range to high-firing clay body (usually blended) and fired to vitrification.

Sulphates: See soluble metal salts.

Tenmoku (temmoku): A high-fired iron-rich glaze (usually fired in reduction) which fires deep black when thick, and breaks into browns and rust colours when thin.

Terracotta: Low-fired earthenware clay, usually red-brown in colour.

Terra sigillata: A finely deflocculated slip coating applied to leatherhard ware and usually burnished and once-fired at low temperatures.

Third firing: The practice of refiring an already glaze-fired piece, usually at much lower temperatures (for lustre, transfers and overglaze enamels).

T-material: An industrial white high-firing clay body with added Molochite; slow-drying and plastic, with good fired strength.

Transfer (decal): A designed or photo image printed in oil-based ceramic inks on specially gummed paper, coated with a lacquer which becomes plastic when dry. The plastic sheet with attached image separates from the paper when soaked in water, and can be attached to the already glaze-fired surface, where it is refired, usually below 1000°C (1832°F).

Trailing: The practice of creating loose linear glaze or slip patterns using a squeeze-bulb or spouted container trailing tool.

Underglaze (painting): The practice of applying slips or underglaze colours to leatherhard, dry or bisque surfaces, prior to covering with a transparent glaze before glaze-firing.

Vitreous engobe: A slip that, when fired, becomes partially vitrified and does not usually require covering glaze.

Wax (resist): The use of liquid paraffin (usually heated) to mask and separate glaze pattern on-surface (much like batik).

Wax emulsion: A water-based wax resist.

Recommended reading

HISTORICAL AND GENERAL

Caiger-Smith, Alan, *Lustre Pottery: Technique, Tradition and Innovation in Islam and the Western World* (Faber & Faber, 1985).

Caiger-Smith, Alan, *Tin-Glaze Pottery in Europe and the Islamic World* (Faber & Faber, 1973).

Carnegy, Daphne, *Tin-Glazed Earthenware: From Maiolica, Faience and Delftware to the Contemporary* (A & C Black, Chilton, Craftsman House, 1993).

Cohen, David Harris; Hess, Catherine, *Looking at European Ceramics: A guide to Technical Terms* (The J. Paul Getty Museum, British Museum Press, 1993).

Cooper, Emmanuel, *Ten Thousand Years of Pottery* (British Museum Press, 2000).

De Waal, Edmund, *Design Sourcebook: Ceramics* (New Holland, 1999).

Ferrin, Leslie, *Teapots Transformed: Exploration of an Object* (Guild Publishing, 2000).

Hess, Catherine, *Italian Maiolica: Catalogue of Collections* (The J. Paul Getty Museum, 1988).

Hopper, Robin, *The Ceramic Spectrum* (Krause Publications, 2001).

Mansfield, Janet, *Salt-Glaze Ceramics: An International Perspective* (Craftsman House, 1991, A & C Black, 1992, Chilton Book Company, 1992).

Ostermann, Matthias, *The New Maiolica: Contemporary Approaches to Colour and Technique* (A & C Black, University of Pennsylvania Press, Craftsman House, 1999).

Scott, Paul, *Painted Clay: Graphic Arts and the Ceramic Surface* (A & C Black, 2001).

Wilson, Timothy, *Ceramic Art of the Italian Renaissance* (British Museum Press, 1987).

TECHNICAL AND PRACTICAL

Beard, Peter, *Resist and Masking Techniques* (A & C Black, University of Pennsylvania Press, 1996).

Constant, Christine; Ogden, Steven, *The Potter's Pocket Palette* (Apple Press, 1996).

Daly, Greg, *Glazes and Glazing Techniques*, (A & C Black, Gentle Breeze Publishing, Kangaroo Press, 1995).

Fraser, Harry, *Ceramic Faults and Their Remedies* (A & C Black, 1986).

Gibson, John, *Pottery Decoration* (A & C Black, Overlook Press, Craftsman House, 1987).

Hamer, Frank & Janet, *The Potter's Dictionary of Materials and Techniques*, 4th edition (A & C Black, University of Pennsylvania Press, Craftsman House, 1999).

Hinchcliffe, John; Barber, Wendy, *Ceramic Style: Making and Decorating Patterned Ceramic Ware* (Angus & Robertson, 1994).

Lane, Peter, *Ceramic Form: Design and Decoration* (A & C Black, 1998).

Minogue, Coll, *Impressed and Incised Ceramics* (A & C Black, Gentle Breeze Publishing, 1996).

Rhodes, Daniel, (Revised and expanded by Robin Hopper), *Clay and Glazes for the Potter*, (Krause Publications, 2000).

Peters, Lynn, *Surface Decoration for Low-Fire Ceramics* (Lark Books, 1999).

Scott, Paul, *Ceramics and Print* (A & C Black, 1994).

Tudball, Ruthanne, *Soda Glazing* (A & C Black, University of Pennsylvania Press, 1995).

Zakin, Richard, *Hand-Formed Ceramics: Creating Form and Surface* (Chilton Book Company, 1995).

Rawson, Philip, *Ceramics* (University of Pennsylvania Press, 1984).

PHILOSOPHICAL AND AESTHETIC

Bayles, David; Orland, Ted *Art and Fear* (Image Continuum Press, 2001).

Brolin, Brent C. *Flight of Fancy: The Banishment and Return of Ornament* (St. Martin's Press, 1985).

Caiger-Smith, Alan, *Pottery, People and Time* (Richard Dennis, 1995).

Coatts, Margot (Editor), *Lucie Rie and Hans Coper: Potters in Parallel* (Craftsman House, Barbican Art Gallery, Herbert Press, 1997).

Flam, Jack D., *Matisse on Art* (F. P. Dutton, 1978).

Forestier, Sylvie; Meyer, Meret, *Les Céramiques de Chagall* (Michel Albin, 1990).

Itten, Johannes, *The Art of Colour* (Van Nostrand Reinhold, 1973).

Koplos, Janet; Borka, Max; Stokvis, Willemijn; Poodt, Jos; *The Unexpected: Artists' Ceramics of the 20th Century, The Kruithuis Collections* (Harry N. Abrams Inc, 1998).

Larson, Ronald, *A Potter's Companion* (Park Street Press, 1993).

Leach, Bernard, *Hamada, Potter* (Kodansha International, 1979).

McCully, Marilyn, *Picasso: Painter and Sculptor in Clay* (Harry N. Abrams Inc, Publishers, 1998).

Paz, Octavio, *Alternating Current* (Arcade Publishing, 1990).

Ramie, Georges, *Picasso's Ceramics* (Chartwell Books, 1974).

Theroux, Alexander, *The Primary Colours* (Papermac, 1996).